BROKEN CIRCUITS

A Memoir of Alzheimer's Disease in Four Voices

By

Marilyn Mehr

with
Nancy M. Snell
Judith M. Olson
Dennis R. Mehr

This book is a work of non-fiction. Names and places have been changed to protect the privacy of all individuals. The events and situations are true.

© 2003 by Marilyn Mehr, Nancy M. Snell, Judith M. Olson and Dennis R. Mehr. All rights reserved.

No part of this book may be reproduced, stored in a retrieval system, or transmitted by any means, electronic, mechanical, photocopying, recording, or otherwise, without written permission from the author.

ISBN: 1-4107-7873-8 (e-book)
ISBN: 1-4107-7872-X (Paperback)
ISBN: 1-4107-9942-5 (Dust Jacket)

Library of Congress Control Number: 2003095848

This book is printed on acid free paper.

Printed in the United States of America
Bloomington, IN

1stBooks - rev. 08/27/03

TABLE OF CONTENTS

INTRODUCTION		vii
CHAPTER ONE	KEEPING AN APPOINTMENT	1
CHAPTER TWO	HANDCARTS AND GENOGRAMS	31
CHAPTER THREE	LOSING AT HEARTS	59
CHAPTER FOUR	DIGGING DEEP	81
CHAPTER FIVE	A GOLDEN ANNIVERSARY	117
CHAPTER SIX	PROTECTING OUR OWN	147
CHAPTER SEVEN	LOSS AND RECOVERY	183
CHAPTER EIGHT	MR. POTTER AND THE NIGHT CLERK	213
CHAPTER NINE	A TIME-OUT FOR MOTHER	241
CHAPTER TEN	GOING HOME	267
CHAPTER ELEVEN	A STILLNESS IN THE HOUSE	285
CHAPTER TWELVE	MOURNING AND REMEMBERING	313
EPILOGUE	A NEW FAMILY-1996	329

No more masks! No more mythologies!

Now, for the first time, the god lifts his hand,

the fragments join in me with their own music.

    Muriel Rukeyser, 1968

INTRODUCTION

As a therapist I have worked with hundreds of families over the past twenty-five years. I have gathered wives and children around the bedside of a retired general dying from lung cancer who struggled to tell his family that he loved them; I have met with a family of Cambodian refugees whose mother could not leave her home, so paralyzed was she by her memories of killing and persecution; I have eaten dinner in a hospital cafeteria with the family members of a young anorectic woman who were so merged that no one could order separately. In almost every instance, the family members were frightened and confused, but were still able to offer support, understanding and love to one another.

Having witnessed the power of these connections, I had not yet been able to form very strong ties with my own family members. In 1984, as a forty-six- year old psychologist who had worked in family medicine for more than two decades, I devoted myself to my work and my partner, Betty. My two sisters, Nancy, forty-four, and Judy, thirty-nine, as well as my brother Dennis, thirty-seven, had all disappeared into their own work and families, too. On holidays and brief vacations, we gathered in Los Angeles, in the home where my mother, who was then sixty-eight, cooked dinner. They had lived here, in a suburb south of Los Angeles since 1942. We joined together at my parents' stucco house, bringing our partners and children, and ate dinner, speaking superficially about our lives. We avoided sharing our deep concerns and feelings—sadness over the loss of a friend, worry about a child's drug problem or even illness in our mates. We turned the pages of the family album, remembering the happy times, passing over the blank spaces concealing secrets we had never shared. Our collective book of memories never really represented the truth of our lives. In this respect, we were probably not too different from most American families near the end of the Twentieth Century.

When a physician called me in 1984, to inform me that my seventy-four year old father had Alzheimer's Disease, I felt frightened and alone. I sat by the telephone in my office for awhile and decided to call my sister Judy, in Texas, then my sister, Nancy, in Utah, and then my brother, Dennis, just a few miles away in Fullerton, California. Cautiously, at first, we spoke about our fears, our worries about Mother and finally, about ourselves. We began to fill in the spaces in the family album.

When I put the phone down, I wondered why I had waited so long to share myself, although I realized that we had all learned the lessons of Anglo-Saxon parents to "keep your own counsel." As the oldest child, I had always been independent and strong, priding myself in my ability to organize and direct my siblings, never willing to reveal my need for help and reassurance. When I stepped outside of my family, I often felt a deep insecurity: my dark hair and olive complexion set me apart my WASP classmates; I was also a Mormon among Protestants; and, I was a smart girl in a working class neighborhood. No one guessed how insecure I felt, seeing only a responsible kid who went to an odd church and always brought home good grades. I also had a wicked sense of humor, exposing the imperfections in almost every one but myself. Later, I discovered my own "imperfections," my lack of belief in my parents' religion, my lack of attraction for the opposite sex, my inability to support the government in an unjust war. Yet, I couldn't share these beliefs with my family. Instead, I pretended to be the daughter they wanted, the responsible, pious child, the good student who eventually went to college, earned a Ph.D. and became a psychologist and a professor in a teaching hospital. I never revealed the real person I had now become and neither had anyone else in my family.

In 1984, there were many broken circuits in my family. My second sister Nancy, the conservative Utah mother of seven children, a Relief Society President in the Mormon church, concealed seething resentments towards my father for past abuses which often erupted in sudden explosions at her own children; the next younger sister, Judy, was also a devout Mormon mother of four, a professor of education at a Texas university and covered her shame over her anger at our mother with an extra hundred pounds; my brother Dennis, the youngest, worked in my father's auto parts business, lived in

Fullerton, California with his wife and two children, laughed, joked, told stories and drank heavily.

As we struggled to help our parents cope with the assaults of Alzheimer's, we came to know one another as the adults we now were. Over the course of the ten years of my father's decline, I expressed my political and religious views and came out as a lesbian to my parents and family; my sister Nancy eventually admitted her hurt and anger at my father; my second sister Judy, acknowledged her frustration with our mother and sought help for her eating disorder; and, my brother, at thirty-seven, began to realize the price of his love affair with alcohol. Of course, each of us had known most of these "secrets," but we had not spoken about them.

Our father's illness was the catalyst that forced us to communicate, to remove our masks and become truly present in the family we had left. As we talked about his care, we also began to talk about ourselves, how our lives had changed, who we were and what we believed. We grew closer and gave up some of the masks of childhood. I gave up "the boss," at least some of the time, my sister Nancy, "the escape artist," my sister Judy, "the doll baby," my brother Dennis, "the jokester." We eventually learned to see one another as complex and interesting people. One day, we were even able to imagine a collaboration which finally resulted in this book. For the past two years, we have written, argued, cried, apologized and forgiven each other, sometimes all within a week. Through this difficult and heart-rending process we have learned some lessons that others may value: that love depends upon honesty and trust; that the injuries of the past can be healed; that a new family can arise from one which has been broken.

Our parents had been unable to teach us these lessons. Their own marriage was a lesson in spontaneous combustion. As children, we held ringside seats to their sparring and teasing, their provocations that inevitably led to explosions and tears. For awhile, a long silence would follow, a punishing withdrawal in which children delivered messages between the aggrieved parents. After a few tense days, some words would be exchanged, a gift delivered, a smile to indicate forgiveness, then a precious time of tenderness and love would transpire. We never knew when the cycle would begin again. We did know that intimacy could be dangerous, that trust made one vulnerable, that love was always followed by hurt. We were like cars on a ferris wheel, attached to the main axis, but constantly thrown into the air and brought back to earth again.

We grew up in this explosive mix of love and rage without understanding either of our parents very well. We loved him, but were terrified of his temper. We loved her, but were angry that she wouldn't defend us from his outbursts. Above all, we tried to maintain fragile moments of peace. We failed. The battles continued and we inevitably realized that our only recourse was to escape. All three daughters went away to college at eighteen, our brother left at nineteen to join the Air Force and we enjoyed affable, but distant, relationships with one another.

Our father's illness forced us to return to our childhood home in Southern California and confront our past. For ten years, we met, attended doctor's appointments with Dad and Mother, listened to their frustrations, tried to problem-solve, and sometimes, just cried with them. We learned not only to talk about the past, but to plan for the future, to discuss the delicate issues of medical care, estate planning and funeral preparations. When Dad died quietly in his sleep, in 1994, in the large airy den attached to the house, we had gradually come to understand our parents. As importantly, we finally understood the meaning of trust and intimacy among brothers and sisters.

We miss him. The house is silent now. His clothes still hang in the closets, his scent still permeates the air, but there is a vast and awful quiet. After he died, we would visit Mother, listen to her shuffle through the rooms, lost, picking up a newspaper, glancing at the headlines and moving on, aimlessly. She misses her grounding wire and she drifts, finding little purpose or pleasure. We asked her to contribute to this book, but she postponed and delayed, unable to face once again the decade-long ordeal of caretaking, the ultimate theft of her self.

To understand our family, the reader must know something about this strange and uniquely American religious sect, known as Mormonism. Why did seemingly rational people leave family and friends to join converts of a peculiar religion on the frontier of the American West? Our grandparents would have answered simply, "We believed in the words of the Prophet," meaning that they were persuaded by the story of Joseph Smith who had prayed at his bedside in upper New York State in the 1830's, seeking to know "the one true religion." According to his claim, he was visited at the age of 14, by an angel who told him that all of the other religions had been corrupted by greed and indifference. The true gospel must once again be restored, and he was to be God's messenger. For three years, the boy had subsequent visitations by the angel who directed him to a large Indian mound where golden plates were stored recounting the history of native peoples on the American continent as well as lost records of the life of Christ. The religion promised salvation to those who believed, followed the words of the Prophet, paid their tithes, attended church, and baptised their ancestors in the Mormon temples. By doing so, families would continue into the next life, a time when mortals could be transformed into gods themselves, procreating and populating other planets. The possibilities for people locked into the medieval class structure of European countries were endless.

As children we were educated in the ways of the Mormon church. As adults, two of us remained believers and two of us didn't. The two middle children, Judy and Nancy became devout Mormon women, while the oldest and youngest, Marilyn and Dennis, left the church but remained connected to a large and extended family of Mormons. Our sisters expect to meet our father in an eternal heaven where souls are reunited. My brother and I still treasure the history of our hardy ancestors, but do not believe that we will ever see our father again. While our beliefs about the religion differ in the extreme, we all agree that right now, we cannot phone Dad, meet him for lunch, ask him for a loan or hear his full-bellied laugh. Despite our differences about the finality of his death, we are learning to know and trust one another.

We have written this book as a history, not in the traditional sense of the recording of a longitudinal course of events, but as a series of crises that changed and deepened a family, We wanted to show how these crises helped us to understand our parents and, ultimately, to forgive them for their limitations. In so doing, we hope to illuminate the process of vulnerability, trust, honesty and intimacy that takes place in our evolution. It is our hope that the families of Alzheimer's victims, as well as health care professionals, will understand that the caretaking process can strengthen families, if the crises brought on by the disease are understood and addressed.

The book will reflect the stages of our family's passage: our gradual awareness that something was "wrong" with Dad; our attempts to barricade ourselves against that awareness as we escape into our own families; our tentative expressions of fear as we realize the seriousness of the disease; our search for support and reassurance from one another; then, the development of trust and honesty as we face the loss of our father; and, finally, mourning and renewal. At the conclusion of the book, we have dropped our family masks and allowed ourselves to be seen as we now are.

In the months following my father's death, my brother and sisters and I formed a spontaneous network of telephone conversations, letters and e-mail transmissions as we recalled family events, exchanged personal memories, repeated funny moments in the family album. As we continued to communicate, I recognized how each of us experienced the loss of our father in a unique way. I knew that if we were honest about ourselves that readers would identify with our struggle. I asked each of them to write about themselves and their memories. My sisters and brother reluctantly began to write, offering their work to me as editor, for review and synthesis. Of course, they were worried, having divulged secrets and vulnerabilities to a potentially large audience. *What will their children think?* Nancy has seven, Judy four, and Dennis two. The opinions of their children matter, just as do those of our mates: Betty, Lee, Jim and Linda. Even so, each of us has been willing to remove our masks and trust that our families and friends will understand our purpose.

As the narrator, I provide a connection between events and people to allow the reader to understand other points of view besides our own. The chart notes of my father's family physician, Ken Brummel-Smith, document the physical signs and symptoms as seen from a medical perspective. My mother's point of view would have offered still another level of insight and experience, but she has found the memories too painful to address. Instead, she has given us permission to use her letters, recall her words and describe her actions. As a musician, she plays the accompaniment to each of our voices, a lone pianist finding the chord that allows each of her children to sing. Our father would have enjoyed our recital.

CHAPTER ONE

KEEPING AN APPOINTMENT (1984)

> Gerontology Clinic, Rancho Los Amigos Medical Center, Downey, California
>
> Date of Visit: Sept. 19, 1984,
>
> Presenting complaint: Patient is a 74 y.o. white male, prefers to be called "Al," accompanied by his wife, Vivian, age 68, who has noticed recent episodes of forgetfulness and disorientation.
>
> History: 1-2 yrs of forgetfulness, making mistakes in use of checkbook, easily distracted and has run red lights frequently. Couldn't pass written driver's license x3, but staff ultimately let him "pass" anyway. Family notices problem often, children more than spouse. Pt denies any problem. No hx of head trauma, strokes, alcohol or seizures, etc. Very healthy all of his life.

> Vital signs: BP 170/92
>   Wt. 217
>
> Psych/Tests: Score on Mini-mental status exam: 20/30
> Plan: Schedule family conference with Mr. and Mrs Mehr and adult children living nearby—daughter, Marilyn and son, Dennis.
>
> (signature) Kenneth Brummel-Smith, M.D.
> Attending Physician

The intercom buzzed insistently alerting me to a message from the front desk of the family practice office. Sitting at my desk, I hurriedly signed a note from a patient's chart and picked up the receiver.

"Hello, this is Dr. Mehr."

"Hi, Dr. Mehr, this is Rosie. A Dr. Brummel-Smith is on line A. Can you talk with him?"

"Sure, Rosie, put him on."

She transferred the call and my friend and colleague, Ken Brummel-Smith greeted me, exchanged a few pleasantries, and then lowered his voice, speaking softly.

"Marilyn, we've completed the testing on your father. His general health is good, but he has some early signs of Alzheimer's. I think we should have a family conference."

I drew in a deep breath, trying to absorb the news. "Sure, Ken. I'll talk to my brother Dennis...the others live out of state...we'll be there."

Our family had resisted an evaluation of my father for nearly two years, wanting to avoid the embarrassment of medical inquiry and probing. As a psychologist I had conducted hundreds of evaluations, hoping that my "objective" evidence would assist families in making good decisions and planning for the course of chronic illnesses. Even so, I avoided recommending an evaluation for my father, until finally, the repeated calls from my mother broke through my denial, like a woodpecker, tap, tap, tapping on the roof until a shingle breaks and the dark contents of the attic are exposed.

It was August 11th, the day after her birthday, that Mother called. I was sitting at my desk when the phone rang. As usual, she masked her concerns with laughter, telling funny stories about Dad that exposed his fallibilities and failings. I hadn't paid close attention to this conversation because I expected the usual catalogue of Dad's childish and amusing antics. This time, the story progressed into a tale not merely of bungling, but of disorientation and chaos. "Your Dad really did it this time," she began. "He got himself lost on his way home from our condo in San Bernardino to Hollydale. His dog was with him and somehow, they ended up in Long Beach Harbor, circling around for two hours until he finally pulled into a gas station and asked for directions. Can you imagine asking for directions to get to his own home?" There were giggles and titters as she recounted his confusion, but I could tell that she was worried.

"Mother," I said firmly. "You've been telling me stuff like this for six months and now it's getting *worse!* Something's *wrong* with him, can't you see it? It's not funny!"

She paused for a few minutes, drew in a quick breath and continued, "Well, I know, but the thought of him driving around Long Beach with all those oil wells pumping and the little dog barking was too much!" Her voice trailed off into a small sigh.

I wanted to be patient, but the alarm bells going off in my head were too loud. "Mom, think about this. He was driving from San Bernardino to his home in Hollydale, a trip he had made at least a hundred times. Why did he drive to Long Beach?"

Mother weighed my question for a moment, and then said warily. "Oh, I guess he must have taken a wrong turn."

"And then made more wrong turns…"

"And forgot where he has lived for forty-five years…" She stifled a small sob of frustration, just a gust of admission suggesting that she knew the storms that lay ahead.

Determined to run away from bad weather, she continued in a "I can't trust him with anything. In June, he lost his checkbook, then he left his watch, you know that expensive one he bought in Paris, in a coffee shop, and he asked Nancy how Brad was doing in school. He *knows* that Brad is Judy's son!" Her voice was tense and angry. "Worst of all is the way he runs red lights."

"Yes, Mom. That's the worst. It's dangerous."

I began to feel as though I were talking to a charge nurse, one that wanted me to know that she had documented every observable behavior of her patient, knew exactly what was wrong with him, but would never ever suggest a diagnosis. As a good nurse, she would observe, make notes, call the physician if necessary, but always refrain from suggesting a direct course of action. My mother's denial of the importance of these "foolish things" annoyed me. This man in the wayward red truck was her husband and my father. There was a reality here that she failed to see. If she were my patient, I could probably "walk by her side" until she gained more insight, but she was my mother, he was my father, and I was frightened.

"Mom, listen...Dad's in trouble and we have to find out what's wrong with him. We can't wait any longer. Dad could get lost, have an accident..." I hesitated, unable to list the darker consequences of our delay. "I'm going to call Ken Brummel-Smith at Rancho Los Amigos and make an appointment for an evaluation."

At last, she stopped giggling. "Okay, fine, but I *know* he won't go."

"Yes," I insisted, "he'll go." Tied or tethered, I thought, he's going.

After a swift goodbye, I hung up the phone and quickly dialed Ken's number. I didn't have to search for a good physician because I already knew one of the best geriatricians in Los Angeles. Ken Brummel-Smith had just become the Director of the Older Adults Section at Rancho Los Amigos. Ken and I had met first at Children's Hospital in 1978, when he was a medical student and I had just become a psychologist. As an intern, he was curious and searching, wanting to join every clinical session, take part in family meetings with anorexics, group counseling with gang members, school conferences with fire-setters. For a short time, we were a team, a model of professional collaboration.

To Mother's surprise, Dad went to all of his appointments with physicians, nurses, pyschologists and social workers, complaining, but responding to their questions. When the evaluation was complete, Ken called me and a week later, I turned the wheel of my car at the sign of a small arrow pointing to the Older Adult section of the Rancho Los Amigos Rehabilitation Center. I was looking for what was described as "a funky old gray Victorian building," where a team of experts had examined my father for signs of Alzheimer's disease. My mother, my sisters, Nancy and Judy, and brother, Dennis, and I would have gone anywhere to find out what why Dad was behaving so erratically, but we didn't have to go far because "The Rancho," as we began to call it, was less than two miles from my parents' home. They have lived in their three-bedroom stucco house in a small suburb southeast of Los Angeles, since 1942, where their four children grew up, riding our bicycles along its neatly ordered streets. As I found my way through the eucalyptus-shaded roads, I was deluged by a memory.

The summer before I was twelve years old, I would strap my three-year old brother onto the back of my Schwinn bicycle and we would race through the dusty streets of the Rancho, flying through the bramble-covered acres of what was then called, the "County Farm." I told my mother that we were picnicking in the park, because I knew we weren't supposed to ride in this rough tract of land where the government had sent homeless men to grow vegetables and look for work. Most of them sat on benches, talking, smoking their hand-rolled cigarettes, and waiting for their lives to improve. As children, we were cautioned repeatedly to avoid these men "because they might hurt you," but I couldn't believe that these broken men could harm anyone, so I took my chances, riding with my brother as he waved to the old men, thrilling at the whisk of the wind across my back. I still felt an old rush excitement as I gunned the engine of my Mazda RX, a single woman in the land of her childhood.

Through the windshield, I saw only a few doctors and nurses in chalky white lab coats walking from the large rehabilitation hospital to its outpatient clinics. The old men in bib overalls no longer lounged on wooden benches waiting for their lives to improve. Now, there was only the crisp, determined march of physicians followed by coveys of medical students trailing their leaders like ducklings. I stopped the car for a moment at the rim of a palm-lined plaza and tried to discern the remains of the old quonset huts and alleyways.

The beep of a car horn startled me and I shifted the Mazda into low and circled the roundabout to the two-story Victorian building where I would meet my family. Over the front porch hung a small wooden sign, "Older Adult Center," the place where my brother Dennis and I would meet with Dr. Ken and my parents. Afterwards, I would call my sister Nancy who lives in Salt Lake, and my sister Judy, who lives in Texas, who would be awaiting news of our conference.

Mehr

As I unfolded myself from my sports car, Dr. Ken approached, smiling and relaxed. Uncomfortable with the formality of uniforms, he wore the clothes of a working man— khakis and a blue denim shirt that mirrored the intense color of his eyes. At thirty-eight, he still seemed boyish and unfinished. His wispy hair and finely polished face appeared youthful and innocent, as though the pain he had witnessed as a physician had not wounded him. He greeted me openly, his gaze full of hope and optimism.

"Hi, Marilyn. Your Mom and Dad are already here...your brother just arrived...they're in the conference room." He embraced me in a tender gesture that communicated the affection we shared. This time, though, he was the doctor and I was simply one of the members of a family needing help.

It wasn't easy being a patient. I, as many of my colleagues, had joined the health care profession to conquer illness. Initially, I wasn't aware of the motivations that drove me to health care, but in reflection, I can see that I've always been the "fixer" in my own family, the responsible one, the psychologist who always knew how to patch things up. Not now. My father, a gnarled and rugged tree-trunk, rooted to the earth for three-quarters of a century, was in trouble and I needed help.

Ken squeezed me to say that it was all right to be frightened. It made sense. Sure, I thought to myself. All I had to do was strip off a layer of professional skin and expose myself, my family and our deepest fears, then allow him to show us the road we must travel. His warm embrace told me he was ready to be our sherpa.

Was I ready to follow? Just walk, I told myself, put one foot in front of the other, don't think about what's coming, climb the steps leading to the front porch and open the screen door into the conference room where Dad, Mother and Dennis are seated in orange plastic chairs waiting to grapple with an unkind truth. Ken opened the door and pulled up two more chairs as I put my arms around Dad and kissed his cheek.

"Well, what are *you* doing here?" he asked, looking straight at me, hoping to hide his confusion and fear.

"Just joining the party, Dad." Come on, I told myself, get real. This is not a party. This is about your father! I took my place in the circle and started over. "We're here to talk about your health, Dad."

He sat up straight in his chair, glancing warily at my brother to determine his complicity in this meeting. Dad's appearance revealed nothing about the extent of his confusion. A passer-by might look through the window and see a stocky gray-haired man wearing horn-rimmed glasses, clothed in a white short-sleeved shirt tucked neatly into Navy blue pants cinched at his waist by a black leather belt with a buckle made from an American silver dollar. If the observer lingered, he would see a simple man in a simple uniform, the same one he had worn every working day for the forty years he had owned and run his auto parts shop in Bell Gardens. Unless the observer were sensitive to slight lapses, he would find nothing remarkable about this man, nor his family meeting with their physician. Yet, we were about to hear some ominous news.

My brother and I avoided Dad's glance. Finding no ally, my father folded his arms across his chest and stared at Ken with an attitude that said, *There's nothing wrong with me, Kid. You got the wrong guy.*

Mom found his stance comical and began to laugh nervously. She covered her mouth with a handkerchief, attempting to conceal her discomfort, and hunched her shoulders beneath the pale blue cardigan sweater draped over her shoulders. Her daily "uniform" had become loose skirts and knit pants of any almost any shade of blue—aqua, royal, Navy, midnight, teal or aquamarine. She had always loved the color, because she believed that only blue would flatter her rosy Irish skin. "If only I could wear 'winter' colors," she often wished out loud to me, "like you. You're so lucky to have your father's olive complexion, even if you do look like a native," the term she used to describe almost anyone who didn't fit into our neighborhood of expatriate WASPS from the Midwest. She loved me, but found my coloring exotic and overly sensual, too similar to the newly-arrived children from the border who dressed in loud fabrics and ate spicey foods.

Sitting across from me in an orange chair, she crossed her legs slowly at the knee revealing her rounded garters rolled around the cuffs of her white ankle sox. Her shoes were plain black sandals, Naturalizers, with an added arch support, I was sure. Even as a young woman when her friends all wore three-inch pumps, she would pull my sister Nancy and me over to the "sensible shoe section," pick out a pair of Enna Jetticks, "C" width, and wear them home on the bus, oblivious to the dictates of fashion. Comfort, not style, ruled her decisions, the legacy of frugal Mormon parents.

As Ken reviewed his chart notes, I stole a quick glance at my brother who had retreated into his own corner, smiling at some joke that was not yet evident. I studied his face, trying to decipher the secret language of siblings, the smirks and eyerolls that we had used as children to telegraph a memory or an attitude. "Hmm," one of my siblings would say, "liver," and roll his or her eyes, while the others giggled at the memory of my first attempt to make dinner when I was twelve years old, and had tried to fry liver. Yes, it had been a little rare, dripping blood onto the serving plate, but was it funny enough to remember for forty years? Or was it just because children laugh at stupid things? I never knew, but in the Michelin of family stories, this one received four stars.

Maybe my brother was amused for the same reason he was always amused lately. He had probably stopped for a couple of beers at Andy's, a tavern on Garfield. I could be laughing, too, with that kind of help, but he always seemed to have "that kind of help." What was it with him, I wondered. Was he becoming alcoholic, or did I just run into him at the wrong time? I'll have to ask him, I thought, making a mental note. Of course, he'll tell me to mind my own damned business, but I'll bring it up, anyway. Another time. For now, we were in this room that seemed to have no oxygen and we needed to find out why Dad was in trouble.

Ken closed the chart as Dad stared sullenly out the window. Mother shifted her weight, while my brother waited and smirked. The youngest child in a family of three sisters, he had played the charming baby brother, the boy who would eventually step into Daddy's business, play, laugh, have fun and drink. He was the same age now as Ken, same height, same lean and muscled body, but hairier than this boy-doctor, covered with wisps of dark fur, his face framed by a full dark beard. What different lives they've led, I thought to myself. I knew I could trust Ken to get through the rough spots of the interview, but wasn't sure I could trust my own brother.

He and I had walked different paths, as well. I went away to college, became a high school teacher, then went back to grad school to become a psychologist. He, too, might have gone to college were it not for Vietnam. In 1967, while I marched down Wilshire Boulevard with my classmates chanting, "Hey, hey, LBJ, how many kids did you kill today?" he was a nineteen-year old Air Force recruit checking signals in an underground nuclear missile silo on the Arizona border. His lonely vigil awakened a slumbering mind, though, and he enrolled in some college classes on the base. When his tour of duty was up, he had married and returned home with a wife and child to join his father's auto parts business.

Dad even offered to help him go to college. He made a deal with his son: a salary and a rent-free house, time off to attend college in return for a forty-hour week spent learning the business. Neither of them had determined when Dennis could leave or how often, making his departure open to constant review. "Just this one delivery, Son, and then you can go class," his father would plead. The delivery might be in Compton while his classes were in Cerritos and soon, it would be too late to go school. After each postponement, he became less interested in trying. The light began to leave his eyes as he stood behind the counter day after day, making jokes and waiting for closing time. Then, he could open up the Coke machine where he stored a six-pack and forget about everything—his early marriage, baby son, demanding father, oil-soaked customers and disappearing dreams.

I watched my brother now sitting next to Dad in this circle of orange chairs and want to ask, *"Why didn't you try harder? Why didn't you take the chance you were given?"* His answer was apparent as he put his arm around my father's shoulder, whispering a shared amusement. He couldn't leave because his father needed him too much. The good son could never leave this father who had gone barefoot on the Utah plains and eaten bread crusts for dinner. My brother must have thought he could make up for the deprivation and heartbreak of this deprived father even if he must sacrifice his own future. As the light slants through the faded window panes, I watched him and realized that in his own way, my brother, too, was a healer. And yet, I felt a deep sadness for him and wished I could put him on the back seat of my bicycle and fly away, back to a time of limitless possibilities.

Ken finally set the chart aside and opened the family conference by addressing Dad first, stating simply the reason for our assembly. "Now, Mr. Mehr, we've come here to try to understand some of the changes your wife and children have noticed in your behavior." Turning to me, he continues, "Marilyn, when you asked me to see your father, you said that he had become more forgetful, gotten lost, had trouble following through on things…"

Dad makes a gesture with both of his hands, palms up, as if to say, *Why bother with this?* There was little force behind the gesture, none of the suggestion of explosiveness and rage that we had learned to read in his movements as children, only a frustrated lunge at the air, like a linesman at a football game starting to call a foul, but not sure of his judgment.

"Wait, Ken, let's stop. Dad, do you understand what Dr. Brummel-Smith is saying?" I asked.

He shook his head in frustration. looking lost and bewildered. "I think all of you are making a big problem here. I don't know why you're doing this."

Ken leaned forward and touched Dad on the forearm, "You don't feel any different, Mr. Mehr?"

"*Feel?*" he looked at Ken like a fish peering out through the glass of an aquarium. "*Feel?* I guess the way I *feel* is useless, just no damn good!"

"Oh, Dad," I whisper as I touch his arm, "Dad, you're not *useless!*"

He blinked feverishly for a few seconds, then began to cry. I put my other arm around him, trying to conceal my own tears, hopelessly trying to soften the impact of the truth he has told. My brother offered us both a handful of tissues, keeping one for himself. My mother didn't shed a tear, watching the scene stoically as though she were at the movies. She saw everything, a thin smile fixed on her lips.

Ken didn't notice her withdrawal, paying attention instead to the three of us who are weeping. "Talk through our tears," he urges us, and eventually we are able to problem-solve, find a few short-term solutions to our father's impairments. He will work a few hours a day at the parts store, calling on old customers for orders, making lists to remind himself of appointments. First, he will need to take a driver's test to renew his license, but he can stay involved with his work and friends. We all agree that this is a good prescription for the present, shake hands with the doctor and emerge into the sunshine of a Southern California day.

As we linger beside my parents' blue Ford sedan after the conference, we make small talk, joking with a father and husband who believes that we are "all making things up." My mother and brother and I pretend that these prescriptions will work; yet, we know that we will never be able to offer a medicine that will convince our father of his "usefulness." Dad has hit upon a truth and we all know it. His whole life has been constructed on the necessary coin of work. When he can no longer fill out orders, add up statements and raise hell with suppliers, he will feel "useless," and he does.

Driving home on a busy freeway, I realized that our family DNA has been imprinted with a belief in the redemptive power of work. Our ancestors have been farmers, weavers, millers and carpenters. They have left no fortunes to their children, only the notion that one must work hard, use whatever talents and opportunities one is given and expect no handouts. My father learned this lesson as the child of immigrant pioneers who insisted that he rise at dawn, rake in the hay, milk the cows, walk to a one-room school house, then return home in the afternoon to continue the unending labor of farming. He would never learn to play golf and we all knew it.

This afternoon. I have watched him admit that he feels useless. Even though his withdrawal from the business has been gradual and deliberate, planned by accountants and lawyers, he has still not been ready to stop working. For the past two years, he has driven his red pickup to the shop, aimlessly sorted accounts and joked with old friends. He tells acquaintances that he doesn't have time for golf because he still has to help his son run the business. "There are lots of things those young guys don't know, yet," he would boast. What he didn't say was that there was nowhere he would rather be than standing behind the counter of his own business selling auto parts to a long line of customers.

There are broken circuits in his life. He has filled the missed connections—loss of job, absence of friends, no hobbies—by taking a few trips with Mother, one to Australia, another to his parents' native country, Switzerland, where he was deeply moved by the richness and elegance of the culture. On the weekends, he would do odd jobs at their second home in Yucaipa, a small retirement village near San Bernardino. *If only,* I tell myself, *they could enjoy each other's company more, he might feel "useful," at least to her.* As it was, he was a nuisance to Mother, getting in her way, resenting her telephone conversations and refusing to pursue activities without her.

She had tried to develop a separate life many years before their retirement. "We have so little in common," she would say. *What about fifty years of living together? Haven't you been able to find something in that time that you both love to do?* I wanted to shout, but I realized that they shared one common interest, their four children and their children's children. My sister Nancy had seven, my sister Judy, four, and my brother Dennis, two, so there were many opportunities to phone, send cards and visits. Yet, in retirement, my parents found rare moments of real companionship. She treated him like a house pet, amusing at times, always in need of feeding, but incapable of sustained conversation.

"We have grown apart," she would sigh, as though observing the San Andreas fault from 36,000 feet. They had never really lived on the same intellectual planet, but their differences became extreme when she finally decided to return to school. I was a college freshman when my forty-year old

Mormon mother picked up the pieces of a long-deferred dream and enrolled in the local community college. She was stunned by her own success and the accolades of her teachers. "I am smart, and I guess I've always been smart, but I just never realized it until now," she once told me in a voice laced with anger and regret.

Maintaining a balancing act between school, family, church and friends, she graduated from a state college with a bachelor's degree and sailed straight ahead into graduate school until she completed her Master's in American Studies, then came home to cook dinner for a man whose reading list consisted of the Book of Mormon, the Bible and Sunday School lessons. Yes, they could have discussed religion, family, friends or travel, but when they tried, they could only argue and spar. She was smarter, they both knew it, and neither wanted her to win the battle and ruin the game. Finally, they gave up trying to communicate. She talked on the phone, he rocked on the back porch and petted the dog, Skipper.

Today, sweet, dear Dr. Ken has tried to explore solutions. "Mr. Mehr, can you still call on customers? Wouldn't that help your son in the business?" We all agreed that he needn't bother to join the Rotary Club or volunteer for a political party because he always registered as an Independent. He was forever the outsider, the son of Swiss immigrants who had not been able to improve their lives in their adopted country. Even his economic success had not assured him a sense of membership in any group other than his church where he secured a place through endless contributions of money and time. The Mormon church had given him respect. Why should he learn to play golf?

As I shifted into second gear and turned north on the Golden State Freeway, I finally saw the sign marking my exit to the Mt. Washington foothills. I made a quick right onto Eagle Rock Boulevard and thought about how much we were tied to one another, my old man and I, each the outsider, critical of those inside the tent, but wanting so desperately for someone to raise the flap and invite us to come inside. Well, I will be invited in tonight, I thought as I made yet another turn onto El Paso Drive, and began the twisting ascent onto Division Street, maneuvering the Mazda into hairpin turns until I came at last to our house extending dramatically over the hillside on two thin cantilevers. I loved the sight of this sleek one-story house, a modernist slice of glass and wood emerging from the dry desert hillside, facing the snow-covered tips of the San Jacintos. I was happy to be home.

Inside, Betty would probably be watching the evening news and waiting for me. We had lived together for fifteen years, shared our lives with friends and families, knew all of the characters in each other's kindred dramas. She would want to know, *What happened at the meeting?* I would tell her and she say that we hadn't told the truth. Whatever we had done would confirm her suspicions that we had avoided being honest with one another. She attributed this failing to our training in the Mormon church. "All those handcarts pushed across the prairies, and for what? A big pile of sand where these guys can hide out with their wives. No wonder you don't tell the truth!" She was a New Yorker, a loud, brash, opinionated, an in-your-face kind of woman who loved a woman from a repressed Mormon family from the flatlands of Los Angeles and she would never fit in and knew it. Her role, as she saw it, was to keep us honest.

We drank tea and talked. I explained right away that I wasn't concerned about myself, that I just wanted to figure out how my dad could feel useful again. "He has to," I insisted "and he'll only get there by working. He'll fall apart unless he works…that's all he knows." But, I really didn't believe he would work again, I admitted. I just couldn't stand to see him cry.

There was only a flicker of reproach in her eyes, as she poured more tea. I knew what she was thinking, that I hadn't been honest enough, that I could have somehow broken through the denial, made them understand that my father was sick, that my mother didn't want to know, would never want to know because she would feel too cheated and that we should all face up to what's coming next. I did not want to hear this speech and tonight, she didn't need to deliver it.

As I tried to fall asleep that night, though, truth kept blinking a light on and off at the edge of consciousness. A flashing headline from the chart note kept appearing: "Mental status 20/30." Those scores are marginal, I admitted to myself, and might suggest some decline, but everyone knows how he plays with doctors. He probably wasn't even trying to answer the questions. *That's probably it*, I told myself as I slipped an arm around Betty's waist and drew her closer, *poor motivation*.

BROKEN CIRCUITS
A Memoir of Alzheimer's Disease in Four Voices

He was just playing with the tester, the old gamester...the score is probably normal. 'Just fooling...this may not be too serious after all.

****

My brother saw the meeting at the Rancho as a confirmation of all that he had witnessed for the past year. When I asked him to write about his experiences, he was hesitatant, claiming "not to be a writer," but finally willing to offer another point of view, "if you think it will help." What follows is his account of our first meeting.

Dennis:

Off we went, my sister and I, she was headed north and I went east, crawling along the Pomona freeway, jammed with commuters edging home to their tract homes inOrange County. If my dreams had worked out, I would have been building their damned houses as a contractor, no longer tied to my father's waist as "the son who took over his dad's auto parts business." But, the stock market took a big nose dive, carrying my money and dreams on its back. If I couldn't be a contractor,

Mehr

I could go back to my father's business. When he started to lose it, I knew I had done the right thing.

The "official version" of Dad's illness at the Rancho meeting just supported what I already knew. It was obvious there was a problem with Dad which wasn't going to go away. I noticed the changes in his handwriting first. His letters had always been perfect, good spelling, clear sentences. Almost without warning, then, he starts writing these strange letters to customers, shaky script, ideas all mixed up. After that, he started making mistakes, big mistakes in accounts payable, forgetting to send checks, sending checks to the wrong customers. What could I do? I asked Mother to help him, which just made him angry—or hurt, I guess. He would sit by the window in his "executive" chair and stare at the traffic for hours. He agreed to stop doing accounts payables, but then he looked at me a few days ago, his eyes kind of filmy, and asks, "What am I supposed to do, Son?" I didn't have an answer.

This man had managed his own business for forty-five years, reconciling every dime. I never checked his work because I knew he was as accurate as a computer. Then, all of a sudden, I received these calls from vendors, telling me they had been shorted. "What's going on, Den? Who's doing your accounts?" I had to admit that my Dad was still working the books, but I would review the accounts. They were right. He was messing up. At first, I just did the work over, never mentioning it to Dad. Then, I had Mother help him and finally, we had to ask him to stop. Great! Now, he stares at the traffic all day.

The Rancho meeting didn't teach me anything new. At least we had a doctor checking Dad out. All I cared about this particular night was getting through all the traffic to my home in Fullerton where I would find a fresh six-pack in the refrigerator. Soon, I could forget all of this for awhile. Hiding? You bet—all the time. It sounds like an excuse, and it was. If I didn't see what was happening, I wouldn't have to deal with it. Or, so I told myself.

***

CHAPTER TWO

HANDCARTS AND GENOGRAMS (1864-1984)

11/15/84—Family Conference: wife, son (Dennis), daughter (Marilyn)

Diagnosis:

1. Memory loss—orientation, attention and short-term memory
2. Borderline hypertension
3. Urinary urgency
4. Possible depression
5. Denial

Genogram:

Mehr

Recommendations:

1. Lose weight (217 lbs.)
2. Increase exercise
3. Return Dec. 20 for psych. testing
4. Memory aids/pt. advised to carry notepad
5. Get a driver's eval.
6. Follow-up 2 wks. in Monday clinic

(signature) K. Brummel-Smith, M.D.

Marilyn:

In the weeks following the family meeting, I was able to stop worrying about Dad and pay attention to my work. In a busy family practice office, there were always patients, residents and psychology interns who asked challenging and interesting questions. "Why doesn't Freddy Salazar take his insulin?" "Do you think that Bessie Rogers is suicidal?" "How can I get Bruce Conklin to stop drinking?" Most of these questions required long-term solutions which most residents found frustrating. Still, we worked together and I could avoid thinking about my father.

When I thought about our meeting at The Rancho, I believed that our "team" had found some remedies for his "absent-mindedness." My father wasn't seriously ill, I reassured myself, perhaps a bit impaired, but he was getting older and some decline was to be expected. He could still drive, after all, spend time at the auto parts shop, enjoy family functions. *Why had we been so worried?*

Still, my mother would follow through on the future doctor's appointments and my brother would insist that Dad renew his driver's license. I might speak to Dr. Ken about a psychiatric evaluation just to rule out the possibility of depression affecting Dad's concentration and memory. We could handle this problem, whatever it was—a little dementia, perhaps, but certainly not Alzheimer's. Any further decline would happen gradually, if at all.

I knew that Ken had taken a family history as part of the medical evaluation and, most likely, had used a genogram to record important events and illnesses. When I called him to ask whether he would send me a copy of the genogram, he was more than willing.

"I thought I might show it to my parents and see whether they would like to fill in more of the details."

Mehr

"What a good idea. A few of my patients have taken copies of their genograms to share with their families. They say they learned a lot about their history."

"We'll see…I never know what to expect from them."

He paused for a moment. "Have you thought about a psychiatric evaluation? Your dad covers his feelings pretty well, but he does seem a little depressed. Some medication might make a difference."

"I'll talk to Mother. Medication only works if it's taken and she would be the one who sees that he takes it."

"Well, let me know. We have a good psychiatrist, Dr. Schneider, and…"

"I'll get back to you. Give my best to Karen."

In a few minutes my telephone rang. I let the message play out and waited for the faxed copy of the genogram. Sure enough, the machine started to print and in a few seconds I had my genogram. I was late for work, but was so curious that I poured a second cup of coffee and sat down at the kitchen table to review the contents. *We've learned a few things about survival,* I thought, as I looked at the ages of my grandparents. All four had lived into their eighties, which meant they had survived two world wars, the Great Depression, the loss of family members and friends. They had stayed active, attended church, enjoyed their children and grandchildren and remained healthy until late in their lives.

Ken had recorded our family's history for three generations. I could see definite strengths on this genogram: many marriages, few divorces, healthy children, and no serious accidents. There were a number of jagged lines, though, indicating friction and conflict, particularly one between Dad and my sister, Nancy. A dotted line showed some distance between Dad and his father. Interestingly, there were no straight lines indicating closeness, particularly among the children—Marilyn, Nancy, Judy and Dennis. I stared at the lines and was consumed by sadness. Why had we allowed ourselves to drift so far apart, I wondered.

I put the faxed paper into my briefcase, astonished at what a simple diagram had evoked in me. In the space of one-page, Ken Brummel-Smith had condensed a history of one hundred years of our family's life. The genogram didn't record the texture of our experiences together, but it pointed to problems, the broken circuits of our lives which we had either ignored or tried to repair and failed. I was determined to use the genogram to help me understand my parents and what had happened to the family that had once been close.

As soon as I arrived at my office, I called Mother and told her that I wanted to have lunch with her and Dad. I wanted to ask them both some questions about Dad's genogram. She seemed pleased and was eager to supply more information.

"I'll find some of my genealogy papers, if you like."

"Maybe we can just start with the genogram," I suggested.

On the Saturday following our conversation, I drove to my parents' home in Hollydale, making the familiar turns along Garfield, then McKinley, and finally Pennsylvania Avenue, where they lived. I parked in the driveway and entered through the back door where I found them seated at the table reading the paper together.

My mother offered a cup of peppermint tea and I pulled up a chair. Digging out the genogram from my handbag, I placed it on the kitchen table in front of Dad.

"What's that?" he asked, adjusting his glasses.

"That's your family history," my mother answered. "It's from your appointment with the doctor at the Rancho."

He frowned, wrinkling his brow beneath the baseball cap that shaded his eyes. "I'm not going back there."

"Where? The Rancho? Why not? They're just trying to help, you know." She pursed her lips and poured the hot water into our cups.

"I don't give a damn. I don't need anybody to tell me what to do."

Her voice turned soft and pleading, the kind of careful tone she might use with one of her children who wouldn't eat parsnips. "Al, you just haven't been active. Dr. Brummel-Smith wants you to lose weight and you can do that. If you'd just walk Skipper and eat more protein."

"The hell with him. I'll eat what I want!" He clenched his fist as though he might pound the table and then realizing his helplessness, like a small bird descending from the sky, dropped his hand into his lap and began to cry.

"Al, what's wrong?" She touched his sleeve, unable to find the words to comfort him. Patting his arm, she tried to offer reassurance, but was confused about how she could help.

"Al, come on, let's have a sandwich. I'll make some melted cheese, you know, the kind you like. We can have some soup, too, chicken noodle. Come on, Honey."

He stood up, wiping his eyes with his handkerchief. "No, thanks. I think I'll go feed the dog."

As we watched him walk to the garage, we were silent, sharing a quiet sadness mixed with a sense of apprehension over Dad's health.

"Mom, let's talk. Tell me again how you two got together."

She seemed to warm to the task. "As you know, we were married on January 3, 1936, in Logan, Utah. We had met one year earlier at the Dansante, a large barn that had been converted to a dance hall where young people came to socialize, dance and, don't tell anyone, drink Prohibition liquor. Well, we danced, dated and got married in the Logan Temple, right in the middle of the Depression."

"That was a vote for the future," I added, feeling relieved that she was enjoying telling her story. Her eyes seemed brighter, the lines in her face less creased. She was a good storyteller and couldn't wait to continue.

"You see, I had wanted to finish college. I was 19 years old and had completed my Freshman year at Utah State, but I couldn't continue because our family didn't have the money." Her eyes reddened and she fought back tears as she recalled giving up her place at school and finding a job at the local telephone company answering calls at a switchboard for thirty-five cents an hour. "Number, please? I asked, hundreds of times an hour, as I connected my cousins, friends, teachers…almost everyone in the entire Cache Valley. You see, I had a job, but I was miserable. I would have done anything to get myself out of that place."

"Did you love Dad when you married him?" I might as well ask the question, I thought. What did I have to lose?

"When I met Al, I didn't really fall in love," she said, looking for him through the kitchen window as though he might overhear her. "True, he was handsome, slim, dark-eyed, and he even owned his own car, a black Ford coupe with a rumble seat." She smiled at the memory. "I admit that I flirted with Al, walking very slowly past the Logan Garment Company, where he worked, on my way home for lunch each day."

"Did he know what you were up to?"

"He acted like he was savvy, but he really wasn't, just a farm-boy from the Uintah Basin and he didn't know a thing about women. He would peek through his office window, but he was too shy to say anything. Later on, after we dated, he told me that he was afraid that I was too good for him. My family had a reputation in Cache Valley. Some of our ancestors had crossed the plains with the Mormon Handcart Brigade in 1857, and that alone, gives you a special place in Mormon community. And then, my father, Roy Reid, was an electrician with Cache Valley Electric and my mother was the Relief Society President of the Tenth Ward. I guess there was some reason for him to feel shy."

"Damned right, I did." We both turned toward the small room leading from the kitchen where Dad sat in his lounger watching television. He had entered quietly from the back room and had overheard some of our conversation. I invited him to join us.

"Hey, Dad. Take a chair and join us. We're talking about you."

"Then I should be the one to tell the truth about all this." He had recovered from his earlier mood and was eager to have our company.

"My parents were poor, not like the Reids," he began. "They came to this country from Switzerland in 1904. My Dad was a misfit and failed at everything he ever tried." So, I thought to myself. *Here's the explanation for those jagged lines.* "He ended up dragging the family, my mother, Lena, my older brother, Charlie, myself and my younger brother, Nephi, to an 80-acre farm in this dusty hell-hole on the Colorado border. My Dad, 'Edward' was his name, had been a textile worker in St. Gallen, and didn't know a damned thing about farming. We almost starved to death out there."

"Why didn't you stay there and help him?" I asked.

"I hated the bastard. When I was sixteen years old, I fought with him and said I was leaving. He begged me to stay, even walked me to the gate, but I'd had enough. I walked five

Mehr

miles and hopped a train to Salt Lake City. I tried a few things, went to San Francisco, lost all my money, then my brother Otto offered me a job at his business, the Logan Garment Company, and I took it."

"Did you make up with your father?"

"Look, the only words he had for me were, 'Go, you damned fool, go. I had nothing to say to him."

"What about your mother? Did she love him?"

"Love? I don't think they thought about it. My father was an orphaned textile worker and my mother was a nurse in a psychiatric ward in St. Gallen. There was no future for either of them there, so when they were visited by two Mormon missionaries who explained the gospel to them, they converted. It wasn't just to escape because they believed in the church, always. Even when they had almost nothing, they paid ten per cent tithing to the bishop." "Yes," my mother added. "They called Utah, their Zion, a place of hope."

"My parents arrived on the same ship in Boston Harbor, then traveled overland by train to Salt Lake City. My Dad was a widower with three teen-aged sons and a daughter, and was lost and unhappy until he met my mother, Lena, who had also settled in Salt Lake. She had found a job in a worker's cafeteria. They were lonely and spoke the same language and I guess they just needed each other."

"Why for, I marry him?' she used to ask me when she lived with us after Grandpa died. I had never told my parents about these conversations, but now seemed a good time to recall them. "When I was a kid, about fifteen or so, I didn't know how to answer her. What was I supposed to say? I just knew she was unhappy with the old man and sorry that she had left Switzerland. She would cry and I would hold her hand, and pretty soon we would share a joke and she would laugh. That's all I could do to help. I wish I had known what to do."

Dad seemed surprised at my concern for his mother. "There was nothing you could have done. I guess the church should have helped them, but they tried. They gave them a tract of land out in Wyoming. Some of their neighbors helped them to build a one-room log cabin where I was born. I'll show you a picture of it, if you like. It's nothing much but they were proud of it. My older brother, Charlie, was born in 1909, then

Mehr

I'm the middle son, in 1911, then my youngest brother Nephi, in 1911. See, there we are on your drawing."

"You all did pretty well, even if you had hard times," my mother observed.

"Yup, we did. Charlie joined the Army, I became a business man and Nephi worked for the Post Office. Maybe you could call Charlie's drinking a health problem, I'm not sure."

'Funny, I thought to myself, how even in families with strong religious prohibitions against alcohol, there were nearly always people with addictions. Uncle Charlie wasn't the only one on this genogram, I could see that, but Dad wanted to continue.

"The cabin was about the size of a garage, with a sod floor and two slits carved into the walls for light. you could look out of those windows and see the Tetons. We were hungry, but it got worse. My Dad gave it up in Wyoming and took us all off to another godforsaken place—Eastern Utah—where we really starved. I'll tell you, I ate so many beans that I hate the sight of them to this day."

Watching him as he told the story of of hardship, finding humor in his deprivation, I liked my father. He seemed to be saying, "This is how life works. Sometimes the crops come up and sometimes they don't."

He wanted to finish the story and I was amazed by the detail he could still remember. I knew that Alzheimer's robbed people of short term memory first. I was glad his past memories were still so clear.

"My folks thought the state would build a canal and bring water to their land. Nope, 'never happened. Why? Politics, probably. One Christmas, the three of us, Charlie, myself and Nephi, were so cold and hungry that we tried not to show our mother how miserable we were. All at once, here comes Captain Abbott, this man from a nearby farm, driving up on his wagon, just filled with things we had never seen: oranges, dried meat, sweaters and shoes. Mother cried, and we did, too. I'll never forget him." Dad covered his eyes with his handkerchief for the second time this morning. "I'm sorry about this. When I tell about this man, it seems like 1922 all over again."

Mehr

    I had heard my father tell stories about his life before, but never with as much feeling. He seemed to welcome the opportunity to speak, particularly about something he could remember well. My mother was surprised, as well, and listened carefully without interruption.

    "In 1927, as I said, I ran away to Logan to join Otto in the knitting business. Every morning, my job was to light the factory furnace at five o'clock, so the warehouse would be warm for his workers. After that, I drew up a work schedule, serviced the machines and supervised the employees. It doesn't sound like much, but I was glad to get the job, especially during the Depression when nobody had work. I was lucky…I had a pretty good salary, bought a car, rented an apartment with some other guys and had myself some fun. I had never learned to play games as a kid, no baseball or football out in the sagebrush, never even learned to speak to a girl at a party."

    He smiled at Mother as though remembering her as a girl.

    "When I met Vivian, I thought she was beautiful. Smart, too. I liked her right away, but I didn't know what to say."

"He still doesn't," she retorted. Mother had been quiet during most of the interview, listening to her husband, occasionally gazing out the window as if to imagine the surroundings he was describing. Perhaps she, too, was surprised that he could still remember many of the details. She smiled and leaned forward, looking directly at Dad.

"You had just turned twenty-five when we met at the dance hall. After that, I would just walk by your office at lunchtime, hoping you might come out. You took forever to ask me out."

"I'll tell you why. There you were, a pretty blonde woman with green eyes and an English name who kept running into me. I notice you, but what do I have to offer her, I ask myself. I quit school in the tenth grade and you come from this family with a sister and four brothers who are all straight A students, captains of the football team, star 4-H winners, who have this attitude that says you are the best. So, even if I have a good job and drive a new Model-A Ford, you're still going to think I'm the son of poor Swiss immigrants." He laughed. "And that was true. I was."

Mehr

Mother nodded in agreement, "He was right about my family. My father was the one who set the standard. 'You'll always be a Reid,' my father told my sister and me. My parents didn't have much, but they were proud of their Irish heritage and had earned respect from their Mormon neighbors. In fact, my mother didn't like Al when she first met him. He was polite and dressed nicely, but he didn't have good grammar or table manners. We liked to read, talk politics, debate philosophy and Al didn't join in those discussions. Maybe you could have, Honey, but you didn't. Still, you had a good job and they wanted me to be secure so they finally gave in and said we could marry."

In a tender gesture, he reached across the table and took her hand. "I'm still glad they did.

I stood up and began searching the cupboards for some cookies, giving them a moment of privacy for their memories. As difficult as all of our lives might become, I wanted to remember this afternoon, the pleasure they took in each other's company, their delight in recalling their young lives.

There was a package of fig newtons stashed in the cupboard which I loaded onto a plate and set on the table.

"Now, Mom, what about the polygamists here? The genogram shows you had two grandmothers. How did that happen?"

Dad started to laugh. "That's right, she's the one with the polygamists in her family."

"Come on, he only had one extra wife. My grandfather was called *Nahum*. and he converted to the Mormon church in 1860. He moved from Pennsylvania with his first wife Rachel and their children to southern Idaho to be with the Saints, and soon he was the new Bishop of their ward. Well, a few years later, my grandmother, Elizabeth, who is twenty-six, went to see her Bishop to ask his advice about which of two suitors she should marry. Her Bishop, of course, was Nahum Porter, who thought about it for awhile and then told her that she shouldn't marry either of them. Guess what? He said that she shouldmarry *him,* instead!" Mother blushed as she tried to stifle her feelings of embarrassment. "He was fifty-three and she was twenty-six."

These polygamous marriages took place in this country just a little more than one-hundred years ago, I thought to myself. Mother believed that the Mormon women accepted these arrangements, but I wasn't so sure.

"Each woman, Rachel and Elizabeth, occupied one wing of the house along with her children, and shared the kitchen and their husband, in turn. Rachel had four children and the families worked and played together until a tragic accident destroyed their happiness. Grandfather Nahum tipped his wagon over while crossing a stream, knocked his head against a rock and died the next morning."

"How did your grandmothers survive?"

"Rachel moved into her own small home, farmed, raisied her own food and made a little money as a community nurse and midwife. She also took in washings which proved to be her undoing. One day, she lifted a heavy load of wet clothes from the large cast iron tub on her porch and her sides literally began to split, rupturing a hernia. My mother, who was only thirteen, found her and helped her into the house. A telegram was sent to a physician in Ogden who arrived the same day. He operated on her on the kitchen table using drip ether as anaesthetic. As Mother used to say, "The operation was successful, but the drugs killed her." Mother became the "mother" of two boys and a two-year old girl."

"No wonder Grandma was always so sad," I reflected.

"She had a beautiful voice, a pure, lyrical soprano, but she couldn't sing away her grief. She had these awful, dark moods that came over her like an angry cloud that hovered over the household for days. As kids, we didn't know what to do. She went to bed and wouldn't come out for weeks. We never knew when she would get sick, and we never knew what made her get well. We just lived through it."

I was tempted to write, "Depression," beside my grandmother's name and perhaps I could have written beside my grandmother Lena's name as well. Life on the priarie had been hard for these women and their children, Mother and Dad, must have been affected. *I* felt that I was beginning feel more compassion for my parents as I understood some of the losses and hardships their own parents had suffered.

I picked up the genogram, wanting to make a comment that might offer my parents some comfort. "You know, this is a pretty healthy family, but one with some hardship and loss. Most of their members have enjoyed good health, had lived long lives and died of natural causes. Dad's parents may have had some dementia, but very late in their lives. At least, they had friends in their church and family members who could help them."

"I hope," said my mother softly, "that we do, too."

"I do, too, Mom." I put my arm around her shoulders. "I have to go now. I'll call you soon."

After several "good-byes," I returned to my car and began my trip home. At the corner of Pennsylvania and Gardendale, I decided to turn left instead of right and traveled a block to a small park with a few benches and swings. I needed a few moments to think and I found an empty bench where I could watch some children playing and reflect upon what I had heard and what it might mean for myself and my siblings.

I was my parents first child, born on a crisp October morning in 1938, on the eve of World War II. As their firstborn, I believe I was loved and cherished. My parents tell me so, and I believe them.

In 1940, the three of us moved to Los Angeles where my father opened another branch of Logan Knitting Mills. Dad found a large warehouse in Hollydale, "the Hollywood of Southgate," where he and Mother bought their first home. There are various stories about why the business failed after two years in a new location. Some said the War effort made it impossible to obtain materials; some pointed to a conflict between managers, one of whom was my father. In any event, the factory went bust, right on the eve of World War II and my father began a long series of jobs that kept him one step ahead of the draft. He drove a milk truck, signed up for welding instruction, sold insurance, then soldered rivets in the bowels of huge Navy carriers being built in Long Beach Harbor. It also helped his draft status to have two more children, Nancy, in 1941, and Judy, in 1945. Once, I asked him why he hadn't simply volunteered for one of the services and done his patriotic duty. He laughed at the absurdity of such a question, "Hell, I didn't want to be killed, that's why!" His allegiance to any authority, civil or religious, was always guarded and self-preserving.

When the war ended, Dad was fired by the shipyards for fighting with a supervisor and found another job working in a service station on Florence Avenue, in Bell Gardens. In 1946,

Mehr

Union Oil tried to force its dealers into buying franchises. Never one to accede to a decree, Dad asked his co-worker, Jimmy Jones, to join him in a new business, Jimmy and Al's Auto Parts, which opened the day after Thanksgiving Day, 1946.

It was the perfect spot at the perfect time. With a post-war economy booming, the neighborhood filled with "pepper tree mechanics," as Dad called them, men from the Dust Bowl, Arkansas, Texas, Oklahoma, who worked on their old cars in the shade of their front yards and had a voracious need for parts and supplies. When the two men disagreed about managing the business, Jimmy moved to another location and Dad became the sole owner of "Mehr Auto Parts."

His fourth child and only son was born in 1947, and Dad was determined to build a business which the boy Dennis could inherit. His son would never feel the shame of running away from his parents in anger. If Al had to work twelve hours a day to build "Mehr Auto Parts" into a successful company, he would do it. Every morning, he arose at 6:00, whistled in a strange, atonal salutation to the day, lathered his face and shaved, then eagerly dressed, started his red truck and stopped for breakfast at Gloria's Cafe where he always consumed the same meal—two fried eggs, three rashers of bacon, a heap of steaming hash browns and coffee. Satisfied and ready, he drove to his business, placed the key in the lock of the front door and began the day, a man at work for himself, a man in control of his own future.

I decided to make another stop. My brother would still be at the auto parts store and if there weren't too many customers, perhaps I could tell him about my day. When I drove up to the yellow building beneath the large blue sign, "Mehr Auto Parts," I could see him behind the counter talking on the phone. I strolled in the front door and greeted the other men at the counter, LeRoy, David, Manuel, who had also worked for my father.

"Hi, Sis. 'Want a Coke?" Before I had time to answer, he went to the soft drink machine and pulled out two cans of cola. "Have a seat by the desk." "You busy?"

"No, not right now. This morning I had ten guys at the counter, all speaking Spanish at once. I can understand them, but I can't speak that fast. Buenos Dias, what's up?

"I wondered what you thought of the family meeting."

Dennis:

My sister likes to throw these easy low-ball pitches thinking you'll just strike at them and she won't have to throw any fast ones. So, what the hell, I went for the first one.

"I didn't learn anything new, but I guess it was all right. I don't know why he wanted to know all that history."

She took a piece of paper from her handbag. *Now what*, I thought, *a pop quiz?*

"This is a genogram of the family tree. I talked to Mom and Dad about it this afternoon."

I picked up the paper and shuffled through my desk for my reading glasses, a special pair from the Walmart rack that made me look Uncle Jeb on the *Beverly Hillbillies*. I squinted at her notes, trying to decipher the markings, then handed it all back with a shrug.

"Genograms? Handcarts? Religious persecution? I don't understand all that and frankly, I never understood why anyone would go through all that suffering just to live in Utah."

I laughed. "I guess it's called *religion*."

"Nah, I don't get it. Why does anyone leave a beautiful village in Switzerland to come to a god-forsaken desert and starve to death?" I covered my mouth to hold back a laugh, "And if you did get off the train and take a look, wouldn't you have jumped back on the train and gone back home as fast as you could? Especially if they gave you some land in some dried-up place where there wasn't even enough water to grow sagebrush. I have to admit, I just don't understand it."

"You know," my sister admitted, "I don't either, but I think I'm starting to."

***

CHAPTER THREE

LOSING AT HEARTS (1985)

> Older Adult Center, Rancho Los Amigos
>
> <u>6/10/85 Summary of Road Test:</u>
>   The patient was given driver's evaluation and training in light, moderate and heavy freeway traffic. He drives defensively, follows instructions well and is a safe driver in all phases of traffic.
>   He was given a driver's road test. He passed with a score of 85pts. Since no more driver's training is indicated, the patient is cleared to drive and the case is closed.   C. Verese, Driving Instructor

<u>Marilyn:</u>

It had been more than six months since our family meeting at The Rancho. My brother and I were noticing more changes in Dad's behavior, particularly after a couple of driving accidents.

Mehr

Both were minor, but involved lapses of attention, failing to stop at a red light, exceeding the speed limit in a school zone, and could have been dangerous to himself as well as others. Apparently, the Department of Motor Vehicles thought so, too, because they suspended his license. He passed a road test offered by the Older Adult Center with flying colors; however, he failed the DMV test three times, and was unable to drive.

When I told my sisters about the accidents, they seemed to think that I was exaggerating. "Everyone makes mistakes," Nancy told me. They had visited our parents during the past year and Dad was at his best. Judy would arrive from Texas and Nancy would from Utah, go to church with Dad, eat at a restaurant, take a short drive with him, and were convinced that there was nothing wrong with him.

I saw these accidents as warnings of Dad's limitations, signs that we should restrict his driving and take advantage of the time we could enjoy together as a family. I called my sisters to see whether they could meet for a long weekend for a family reunion in Bear Lake, Utah. Both of them agreed, although my brother avoided answering. I finally called him.

"Den, are you going to this family reunion or not? I just need to know to make reservations."

"Look," he protested. "I don't want to go to any kind of reunion. I'm not a joiner. 'Never have been and 'never will be. And you'll never catch me in the Great State of Utah again, no matter who gets married, who gets buried or who has a reunion."

"Yes, but are you going?"

He chuckled. "I've tried to be a good son, run my old man's business, take his shit and bad temper and hold my parents' marriage together, but I'm not a Mormon anymore and I'm not setting foot in their territory."

"I guess that means you're not going."

He hesitated for just a second. "Right, just don't let him drive. I know he passed the DMV test, but I wouldn't let him drive my car."

"Well, how did he pass the test then?"

"Don't tell anyone or you're chopped liver. He failed the test at the DMV three times, but I couldn't stand to see him grounded and I didn't want to be the one to pull the keys, so I made a call to a friend in the Department of Motor Vehicles and called up a favor."

"Den, you know he's had these accidents."

"Sure...why don't you drive him around Bell Gardens, then."

"I don't want to do that, but I don't want him killing himself."

"Do you think I do? I was the one the Emergency Room called when he ran that little truck through a bright red light and crashed his car head-on into a brick wall. I was the one who saw the hard old German lying flat on his back on a gurney, his head laced with black stitches, his eyes all hollowed out. How do you react to a father who has *never* hurt? He reached for me. I know I should take his license, but I can't."

"Then I will. Just don't let him drive."

"Okay. Have a good time in Utah. Now, maybe I can go back to running a business."

We may be shouting at one another, but at least we're talking, I thought. That must represent some progress. We've also agreed that Dad won't drive and can figure out his transportation later. For now, there was a reunion to plan.

BROKEN CIRCUITS
A Memoir of Alzheimer's Disease in Four Voices

In honor of my brother's absence, my sisters and I decided to call our gathering the Partial Reunion and invite all of the grandchildren as well as Mother's sister, Gladys, and her husband Hugh. Judy and Jim would fly to California and drive back with our parents, while I would fly to Salt Lake where Nancy would meet me. Judy remembers her experience vividly.

****

Judy:

Both Marilyn and Mom had called me about Dad's "accidents." I listened as Mother railed at him over his driving, but I didn't take it seriously. It wasn't clear to me until we traveled with him to Utah in the summer of '85, that he wasn't just teasing or playing games.

My husband Jim and our twelve-year old daughter Heather were bicycling together down the coast where they would meet me and our other three children in Los Angeles. I was jealous of their time together, Heather and Jim, but knew that I was too heavy to participate in such strenuous activity. I've never been a sports-lover and as I gained weight and got older, I found it even more difficult to do any kind of physical activities.

I've probably participated in every kind of program for weight loss ever imagined, but every time I would lose twenty pounds, I would gain another forty. Over time, I gained a hundred pounds more than I weighed at my wedding. I didn't feel that I was physically unattractive and I wasn't jealous of Heather who was trim and youthful, but it bothered me when I felt that I couldn't do something that I wanted to do. I finally feel that most of who I am is not the package and I'm pretty comfortable with who I am. I'm just never going to ride a bicycle for eight hours down Highway 1 with my husband and daughter.

We all joined Mom and Dad in L.A. and drove to the Utah/Idaho border in two cars, changing our seats after each restaurant break to share stories and visit. Somewhere between Barstow and the Nevada border, we stopped at a coffee shop for a rest. While Dad was in the restroom, Mom mentioned that something was wrong with his memory. "He's messing up the accounts payable at the shop, losing track of things at home and driving like a nutcase." She laughed as she told us the stories, bouncing her tea bag back and forth in the cup like a metronome, and looking at the restroom door to see when Dad might return. Suddenly, she stopped talking, leaving a touchy silence just as Dad approached the table.

Jim and I nodded sympathetically, trying to act as though we had been engaged in a fascinating conversation. We glanced at each other across the table with raised eyebrows, acknowledging that neither of us would put much stock in Mother's reports. Jim thought that our family always exaggerated Dad's behavior.

"Why is it that all of you Mehrs just love to get together and tell stories on your Dad?" he would ask me. "Either he has lost his temper, turned the sprinklers on a neighbor, or told off City Hall. Whatever it is, he always ends up looking childish or stupid."

At first, I was shocked by this supposed insight and irritated that he had been making mental notes on our behavior. Then I started listening more closely to our conversations. Nance would begin, "Could you believe what he told Jo Sorkness after church?" Then Marilyn would add, "Keep your hands off me, Lady, or I'll report you to the

Bishop!" And Nancy would add, "Too late, she had already smeared lipstick all over his head," to which Denny began crooning, *Red-Roses for a Blue Lady,* leaving us all giggling and falling all over each other.

The whole routine made Jim sick, but I always found it instructive. By repeating these stories in concert, we seemed to be teaching one another lessons in control. By laughing at him, we could overcome our own fears of his white-hot flashes of temper, his childishness and his mood swings. Reporting his outbursts gave us some small advantage. If dark clouds were moving towards the house, we could sometimes prepare for a thunderstorm. *Feed the tiger, soothe the tiger...*I would say to myself.

In spite of our tag-team storytelling, Jim felt more comfortable in my parents home than I did when I was growing up. At the little stucco house on Pennsylvania Avenue, when we first met in 1962, he and I had flirted, shared our homework assignments and, eventually, fallen in love. It was here that he had received the missionary lessons and eventually decided to join the Mormon church. He loved me, my church and my parents, and particularly, my Dad.

BROKEN CIRCUITS
A Memoir of Alzheimer's Disease in Four Voices

I never loved Dad the way Jim did. They were buddies, joking and laughing together in a way that I envied. Jim saw similarities between the two of us, father and daughter. "You were like mirror images of one another—the same dark, smooth skin, the same round face, the same intolerance for fools, the same twinkle in your eyes. You shared your love for the church and felt the same compassion for suffering, and the same concern for your families," he told me later. Sure, but he never saw how dangerous Dad could be when the love was withdrawn, when you might disagree with him and become the object of his blind and sudden wrath. Dad reserved this dark side just for us, his family, showing only the good-hearted, warm and generous self to his in-laws and friends. Of course Jim loved him without reservation or fear.

My husband and father acted like adolescents when they were together, even when they barely knew each other, jostling and kidding, playing cards and telling jokes. Whenever we returned to California, Jim and Dad would play Frisbee with our German Shepherd, Sabrina. Dad would chuckle as she leapt into the air trying to please him. Finally, when her tongue dropped out with fatigue, he would stop the game and pet her, then lead her back at the house where he would carefully mix a huge scoop of dry dog food with a can of high-priced Alpo, then watch her happily as she gulped it all down.

Later in the evening, Jim and Dad often drove to Paramount or Downey to play billiards, drink Pepsis, and tell stories about people and politics. They became close friends, sharing a kind of camaraderie that I never found with Dad. There was always a tension between Dad and me that I couldn't address. I think he was angry at me for growing up, no longer being his little girl in the red taffeta dress, but I didn't know how to talk to him about this. He was the father, after all, and I was angry that he shut me out. I was angry at Jim, too, because he refused to accept my anger at Dad, always reassuring me that he was such a nice guy.

Jim loved Saturday nights at my parents' house. During the sixties, Dad invited a group of friends from the church for a "Men's Night Out," a gathering in the guest room where they all played "Hearts." Now and then, a few women joined in as players, but this was a time when the women hadn't begun to claim their place at the table, either in the game room or the board room. Many of the elders from the church joined the games, even men who had been my Sunday School teachers—Claudell Empey, Jack Morris, Glenn Robinson, sometimes my brother Dennis, and often my sister Nancy's husband, Lee. Dad was the constant, setting a tone of raucous laughter, good-natured ribbing and lively storytelling. Dad was good at the game because he was smart and could take a careful measure of other people. He was a risktaker who could count cards, remember tricks, plan ahead and cut losses. With childlike relish, he could dump his hand on an opponent and leave him speechless! He was unbeatable.

On our trip to Bear Lake, in 1985, when Mother started telling stories about Dad, neither of us believed her. In fact, Jim even asked Dad if he wanted to drive the car for awhile. We were on Interstate 15, near Cove Fort, Utah, when he turned the wheel over to Dad. Sure enough, it was clear that nothing was wrong with him. He handled the car as badly as he ever had—alternately accelerating and braking every ninety seconds at seventy-five miles an hour, chuckling at stupid jokes, glancing from side to side, changing lanes without signaling and cursing any driver who got in his way. Nothing had changed. Dad was still Dad, after all...a little careless, but in control.

Mehr

At least, we thought so until we arrived at Bear Lake that evening. During a late game of Hearts in the condominium, I began to realize that maybe Mom was right, that something was wrong, that Dad was not himself, I sensed it, but Jim saw the changes over the card table and came to bed that first night and woke me up. "Something's wrong, Sweetie. He's not himself," he said as he wrapped his arms around me. "The whole game started off okay...we dropped the two of clubs from the deck...dealt each other seventeen cards apiece. As usual, your Dad short suited himself in clubs...a few hands, then he took the first heart. He caught us by surprise when he led out with the Queen of Spades, the "Old Bitty," as he called her. Lee and I thought he was loaded with spades and hearts and he was gonna' "shoot-the-moon," you know, take all of the tricks. He's pulled it off plenty of times in the past...I knew I wasn't going to be able to stop him because all I had was a bunch of clubs, some useless diamonds, and a few low spades."

Jim leaned closer to me speaking softly. "I thought, *Damn, I'm going to be done-in,* and then I waited for Al to do his number on us and end up with that "shit-eating grin" of his." He paused for a moment, drawing in his breath. "Then, he did an odd thing. After taking the Queen of Spades, he led out with the two of Hearts. Lee and I looked at each other and started laughing because we thought he was making a joke. We knew he would pull back the Queen, exhaust his spades, and finish us off with all of his hearts. But he wasn't joking. As we laughed and accused him of trickery, a befuddled look came over his face. I realized at once that he didn't know what he had done. Leading with the Queen of Spades and following up with the two of Hearts is a prescription for disaster. Lee and I looked at each other again…We realized that Al had forgotten how to play." My husband began to cry and we held each other for a long time, crying together, as we let in the truth…we were starting to lose Dad.

****

<u>Nancy</u>:

I still harbored my own resentments towards Dad, but I knew that the gathering was important to Mother, so I agreed. Besides, I lived close to Salt Lake City, just over a hundred miles from our reunion site.

Mehr

I wasn't going to this reunion to see my father. He and I have never gotten along with each other—we were both too sensitive to put up with other people's judgments. So, I came to Bear Lake to enjoy my children and their cousins, period. Now that my older children were in their teens, I loved to watch them play in the water, strapped to giant dinghies which their dads pulled with churning motor boats. Judy and I watched our kids, trying not to hold on to them too tightly, especially to our youngest sons, Brad and Joseph. Speaking of brothers, my brother Dennis always seemed to turn up missing at these events. We tried to convince him to come by telling him he would be near the Idaho border and could cross over if he needed "space" from family—or a drink—but he didn't take the hook. He wanted none of it. There were still quite a few of us, twenty-four in all, when you count my kids, Judy's kids, some of their spouses as well as their kids. Uncle Jim and Aunt Marilyn, our "heroes," sported the money for wave cutters and jet boats so everyone had a great time on that vast and wonderful lake.

As I watched from the shore I thought of our other reunions, when I was a child and Mom's family all gathered here. The highlight of the week, as I remember it, was always the *battle royale* staged by my mother's brother, Clair, and his wife Jenna Lou, who drank more than they could handle and shouted accusations at each other across the campfire. Grandma Reid would distract us from the main event, wrapped in her flowered apron, offering us copious helpings of barbecue, fresh corn, string beans, peaches and, of course, raspberries! How we loved those bright red berries strewn over cereal, mixed with ice cream, or even fresh from the bowl.

This year, another generation gathered and Dad and I sat beside each other at the dock, calling to grandchildren, waving at the gulls. When the wind began to blow storm clouds over the lake, Marilyn and I offered to walk back with him to the condo where we were staying. The sky darkened quickly and he began to mutter to himself that he didn't know, "What the hell I am doing." We told him not to worry because we knew where we were and could guide him home. Suddenly, it started to rain furiously, drenching the three of us in a crushing cloudburst. My sister and I both tried to protect Dad with our jackets, but we couldn't really run to shelter because he was too unsteady, vulnerable to a quick stumble and fall. We held his arms, steering him to our condo. When we arrived, he was drenched, cold, and shaking uncontrollably. He seemed so frail. I let Marilyn and Mom change his clothes and put him to bed because I can't stand to see him so exposed and weak.

As suddenly as the rain started, it stopped. I settled into a wet lawn chair and watched a rainbow arc across the lake, trying to calm myself. This was a new Dad, all right, one I wasn't prepared to see. A little later, I got up and went into the bedroom looking for my wallet. I stood for a few minutes beside the bed, watching him sleep, wrapped in covers like a newborn. At that moment, I begin to feel a sense of forgiveness for some of his cruelty and rage. He had wounded me emotionally many times throughout my life, but after all, he had been hurt, too, I told myself. He had given what he could, twelve hours a day, every day, to provide the "good life" for his kids so they wouldn't ever have to know the poverty he had experienced. 'Too bad he had to be so sensitive and nasty at times, but I've been the same way myself. Watching him drift into sleep that afternoon, I began to understand this "raging bull" in a new light.

BROKEN CIRCUITS
A Memoir of Alzheimer's Disease in Four Voices

****

<u>Marilyn:</u>

I organized this reunion because I'm the oldest child and mostly, I enjoy the role. Not only did I assign lodging and food preparation, I also directed the Saturday evening's entertainment, the "No-Talent Talent Show," in which everyone had a non-starring role. Nancy and I re-created our childhood tap dance routine, singing and tapping in alternating rhythms to "Sam's Song." In tribute to a childhood performance in which I forgot the steps, I once again lost my place while she followed my missteps, smiling and shuffling to the music. Everyone laughed, including me, and we quickly exited stage left to a round of applause.

Our parents, as well as my mother's sister, Gladys, and her husband Hugh, were assigned the roles of the wise old storytellers, recounting family history and sharing genealogy charts. When they finished, we asked Dad to tell us about his boyhood in the Uintah Basin, expecting that he would recall his adventures with Ute Indians or his fear at being tracked by a mountain lion. He began telling everyone about Willie

Mehr

Sespooch, his Indian friend, who rode behind him on his pinto pony over the dusty plains. Suddenly, he seemed to drift, stutter, then fall silent. I tried to tape the story together, telling everyone about Dad's mother Lena, how she fed the Utes and tried to make a home for her sons.

Hearing his mother's name brought him to attention. "Who are you talking about, Mother?" he asked me.

"Yes, Dad, what a good person she was."

"Well, she *was!*" he gasped, his eyes wet with tears. He began to cry, softly at first as he tried to cover his eyes and then in great sobs, uncontrolled and anguished. Mother sat across the room from him, her arms folded in her lap, seemingly unmoved. I wrapped him in my arms as I, too, began to weep, joined by other members of our family, as well as, Aunt Glad and Uncle Hugh. We wept for our Grandmother Lena, but we wept most of all for our father and ourselves. He seemed like a passenger on a train slowly departing the station for a land where there were no fixed landmarks or boundaries.

We were grieving as a community for all those we had lost, but more so, for those we would soon lose. Without speaking, we all shared an almost tribal connection with one another, a profound link with ourselves, our ancestors, the ghosts who pushed handcarts in the hot mid-day sun. And then, we cried for Dad.

My mother, awakened from her stoicism, and stood up, declaring that we should all sing. One of the nephews found a portable keyboard, hooked it up and set it on a table in front of her. She turned up the volume and played from memory, a rousing chorus of an old Mormon hymn, "Come, Come Ye Saints." We knew the words. We had sung them since childhood.

> Come, Come Ye Saints, no toil nor labor fear,
> But with joy, wend your way.
> If hard to you, the journey may appear
> Grace shall be as your day.

As I sang the pioneer anthem I had learned long ago, I drew nearer to those in the room and to the other ancestor-spirits who hovered in the dark just beyond the box elder trees. They were humming in the night air, those weary souls who had pushed their handcarts all the way across the Great Plains to the Salt Lake Valley. Tonight, we were all those "peculiar peoples," as Mormons call themselves, as immigrants to these

these deep valleys of love and loss. In this moment of singing and recollection, I knew who I was—a Mehr, a Reid, a Schwartz, a Porter, then a Jessup, then a Bisbee, then a Shaffer, then a Page and a Truninger. As we sang together, we all knew for a moment who we were. Then, slowly, ever slowly, the music faded and we all went quietly to bed.

The next morning, the sun rose early over the lake. I couldn't sleep, so I decided to take a walk. There was a coffee shop I had seen earlier, named Polly's, and I was pretty sure I could walk the distance to it. About twenty minutes after I left, my brother-in-law Jim drove by in his rented Ford with my father in the passenger seat.

"It's another mile to 'Polly's.' 'Sure you want to walk?" Jim called out.

I wasn't at all sure that I did, so I jumped in the back seat and joined them. After breakfast, Jim offered Dad the keys to the car, knowing that he shouldn't drive, but unwilling to hurt his father-in-law's feelings.

"You want to drive, Al?"

Dad held the keys in his hand for a long minute, looking out over the lake, beyond the violet hills toward the land of his birth, Wyoming, then shrugged slighty and gave the keys back to his son-in-law.

"You drive, Jim. We'll sit in the back seat." He opened the door for me, bowing slightly. An observer might have seen us chauffeured along the highway, a country squire and his unmarried daughter, enjoying a morning ride along the lake, holding hands and savoring the sweet abundance of the morning.

***

CHAPTER FOUR

DIGGING DEEP (1985)

> 9/20/85
>
> "What is most marked about Mr. Mahr (sic) and his wife is the profound lack of appreciation he has for his memory deficits. He denies them totally. He rationalizes and tends to come up with numerous reasons why he may not remember something. When confronted, he will become anxious and agitated, and these represent small catastrophic reactions.
>
> Of equal or greater concern, his wife does not fully appreciate the extent of his memory impairment. She often attributes his forgetfulness to just plain orneriness. She tends to contribute to his denial and rationalization. Together, they both demonstrate a good deal of nervous laughing and uniform denial of several symptoms."
>
> L. Schneider, M.D.
(Psychiatrist)

Mehr

<u>Marilyn</u>:

Ken Brummel-Smith had recommended a psychiatric evaluation nearly a year ago, but I had postponed urging Mother to schedule one, believing that Dad was functioning well in a familiar setting and there was no reason to disturb him with more psychological probing than was necessary. However, the accumulation of his accidents, his disorientation at Bear Lake and his general withdrawal from work and church, made it obvious to me and others that further professional advice might help.

Upon my urging, Mother made an appointment for Dad him at the Rancho Clinic, then waited for two hours while a psychiatrist, Dr. Schneider, interviewed and evaluated him. I met them at a coffee shop shortly after the appointment where I found them in the entryway searching the tables, Mother looking tense, Dad angry. Sliding into a booth, chewing his lip, he let loose with all the fury he had contained for two hours.

"Goddamned head-shrink! Two hours playing games, asking me my name, the date, who's president. Who the hell cares? Then, little tricks like counting backwards from one-hundred. Does he think I'm a child?" He pounded his fist on the table, then glared directly at me? "Whose idea was this anyway?"

I swallowed hard. "It was mine, Dad. I'm worried about you…Mom is, too. You didn't seem to be yourself at the lake?"

"What lake?" There it was. I couldn't underline the obvious, but Mother could. She began to squirm.

"Bear Lake, Al. You were there in July. Don't you even remember that far back?"

This time, I squirmed. After so many years of fearing him, she had an opportunity for revenge. She would still perform her duties as a wife, taking care of him, driving him to appointments, handling his responsibilities at his business and cooking his meals, but now, she was in control. He would always know when he had slipped.

I had never known how to respond to their anger. After all, I wasn't their therapist, I was their daughter, one caught in the crossfire of interminable arguments and taunts. I wanted them, finally, to love one another, at least, to stop inflicting pain. We hurriedly finished lunch and I told my mother I would talk to the psychiatrist.

Mehr

Seeking some clarification and possibly, support, I called Dr. Schneider that afternoon, explaining that I was both a psychologist and the daughter of his patient. His voice was cordial, but cautious.

"Both of your parents are denying these changes completely. This defense may protect them from the grief they are bound to experience, but it will also prevent them from making necessary plans for the future. They should, for example, be arranging their finances, wills, power of attorney, and seeking some respite care to relieve your Mother. First, they must confront their denial. Can you speak to your mother?"

I agreed to try. She dropped Dad off at the auto parts shop and met me over another lunch at a Chinese restaurant. She talked about the menu, the waiters, the other customers, then told me some new stories about my father's forgetfulness. I tried to stifle my impatience, bringing the conversation back to how we should all make plans for the future, how Dad's illness was not just manipulation, but a physical impairment.

"No one knows why, but the brain develops these tangles that gum up the cells and make people forget."

"I know. The doctor explained all that."

"Then you know he won't get better?"

"Yes. Do you want a fortune cookie?"

If she needed time, she needed time. "Okay, let's have a fortune cookie."

"Here you go," she offered. "You take the first."

"All right," I crack open the cookie and read aloud, "Teach an unskilled mind to sing the feelings of the heart."

"Oh, that's a nice one. That sounds just like you, a teacher. And now, mine." She took the remaining cookie and slowly broke it apart. "If you cannot bear the sound of the cuckoo your journey will never end."

"Oh, Mom," I said, the tears welling up in my eyes. "You can't do this alone. You need help."

"Yes, I can, and no, I don't want any. I don't need strangers banging on my door, going through my things, giving your father a bath. I'll take care of him, myself."

In the weeks following our luncheon, I try to imagine who was writing for the fortune cookie industry. "The sound of the cuckoo?" and "Teach an unskilled mind to sing?" How could they have known? Could they also teach us how we will

Mehr

all cope with our feelings when we do stop denying? Mother had learned to cover up her feelings from parents who had grown up scratching together whatever meager resources they could to survive through the Great Depression. Their own parents had travelled across the country in covered wagons, fifteen hundred miles across the prairie. *See what she was given,* I tell myself. *Then you will understand.*

Still, someone had to look at reality. I was a psychologist and I knew there were tools that could unlock some of the impairments of the mind. I asked Dad to sign a release of information form which I sent to Ken with a request for a copy of his Bender-Gestalt exam:

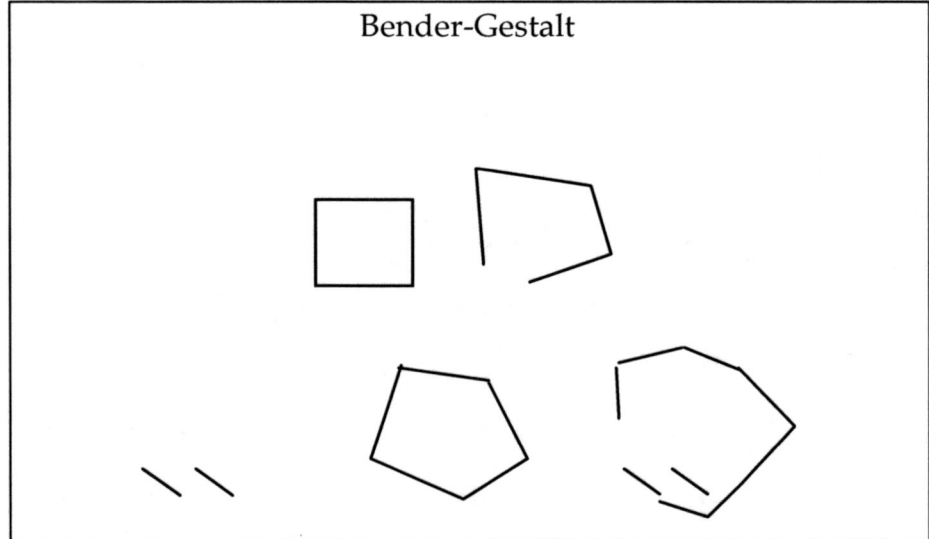

BROKEN CIRCUITS
A Memoir of Alzheimer's Disease in Four Voices

The Bender-Gestalt test attempts to discover perceptual difficulties by analyzing drawings of objects made by the patient. Dad's drawings suggested some serious impairment. These limitations were supported by his other tests, the Mental-Status Exam and several interviews. As a daughter, I still wanted to believe thatThe Old Gamester was just playing a few tricks. As a psychologist, I knew that my father was losing his capacity to remember, to learn, to reason and to perceive. In short, he was losing the capacities that define his personality.

This man who could no longer draw a straight line on a Bender-Gestalt, the middle son, Alma, named for a warrior-prophet from the Book of Mormon, had been the hero of his parents' dreams. As the captain of his own business, he had driven his employees relentlessly. expecting every drop of sweat and every ounce of loyalty he could exact. At home, he had held on to his wife and children fiercely, always demanding their fixed attention. Whatever had happened in his life, he was always in control.

And now, he was losing it. If we were able, we would take care of him, his children and his wife. With all his rages and outbursts, he had still given us enough to enable us to to repay him. None of the four of us knows the spark that caused us to look backward, but each of us began to recall memories and to share them tentatively, at first. We talked mostly by telephone and then wrote to one another, recalling, expanding, gaining insight and getting to know each other. Some of our recollections follow:

The first child of a young couple, I was named Marilyn, after my mother's best friend. No one doubted, though, that I was my father's child. Everyone remarked on our physical resemblance to each other. "Al, as long as she's alive, you'll never die!" He carried me around in a small wooden box like a puppy. We were children together, he and I, learning how to ride a bike, throw a baseball, build a hut in the backyard and shoot pellet guns at the back fence. I knew I had a special place in his heart, his pal, the one who was almost his twin, the one who called him, "Daddy-boy."

Yet, I was a girl and I also resembled my mother. Each seemed to require a copy of themselves, a sign of their worth and significance, and I learned to reflect their deepest wishes whenever I was in their presence.

BROKEN CIRCUITS
A Memoir of Alzheimer's Disease in Four Voices

Reassuring each of them of my loyalty became a never-ending task. *How can I mirror one image without excluding the other? And how do I find reflect my own light?* These are questions I've spent a lifetime answering, a constant searching for identity. As a teen-ager, the pressures to choose intensified. *Who am I? Do I dress up and wear lipstick? Do I join the Deb-Teens and learn ballroom dancing so I'll be more popular?* "Always find out what *your date* is interested in and act as though you're fascinated when he talks," my mother advised me. I tried to please her, but I wasn't really interested in most teenage conversations, either by boys or girls. My mother enrolled me in a social club, but I couldn't wait to get home and read the Edna Ferber novels I loved more than dancing with boys in a rented hall in Southgate.

Finally, I graduated and went away to a Mormon school in Utah, named after the prophet, Brigham Young. On my own, I could skip all of the dances and read as many novels as I wanted. Of course, I majored in English, then found my first real friends who also loved to read. Fellow English members and rebels, we met in underground coffee houses where we read Ginsberg and Ferlinghetti aloud and longed to escape from Utah. By the time I was a senior, I was editor of the campus literary magazine and a prime target for the Campus Cleanup Crusade, a zealous effort by returned missionaries to root out all lax Mormons. I agreed to see a counselor if they would stop monitoring my activities. They agreed, I talked to a counselor, and I graduated in 1960.

After a summer at Radcliffe, I came back to L.A. for a scholarship at U.S.C. which trained me to teach in the inner city of Los Angeles. Part of my preparation required me to observe a "Master Teacher" for three hours a day, learning through the observation of good teaching. Miss Buchanan was unlike any English teacher I had ever known. The others had been dull, drab and humorless. She was smart, chic and funny. I fell in love with her.

At last, I began to understand the desolation of the Debteens years. I wasn't a wallflower, although perhaps a "malfleur," as the French say, the lesbian, the dyke, the queer. I loved Miss B, not only as a brilliant teacher, but as a sexy and alluring woman. What I felt for the first time was *passion*. I couldn't have her because she had a lover, as I eventually found out. So, I would find someone like her, I decided. What followed was nearly four years of acting like the adolescent I had never been. At twenty-four years of age, I started drinking, smoking, going to bars, having sex and loving it. All of this frenetic activity concealed a mass of insecurity I still had not confronted. When a friend suggested a therapist, I was ready.

One of the wise people I have had the good fortune to meet was the therapist I saw for the next five years. Her name was Winafred Lucas and she saw patients in a small suite of offices near U.C.L.A., in Westwood Village. She identified my turmoil, helped me to keep from destroying myself through my own excesses, and waited patiently while I came to know myself. Actually, she did more than that. She encouraged me to dream about a professional life beyond teaching high school, believed that I could become a psychologist, and that I could find a partner who would add richness and fulfillment to my life.

Two months before my thirtieth birthday, I quit teaching, returned to grad school and met Betty Walker. I noticed her in our Counseling Seminar, and admired her quick wit and intelligence, but I was sure she was married, lived in Altadena with a dog and two kids. Unexpected things happened in that room, though. We were all swept up with the idealism of the sixties. arguing about the War, starting women's groups, debating existentialism. In this heady climate, many love affairs began, but I never expected that mine would be with her. She was everything that I was not—sophisticated, worldly, brash—a real New Yorker. And I was all that she was not—quiet, reflective and dreamy—a true Californian. We were drawn to each other at once.

At first, I was secretive about our love, not wanting to crack the role of good-girl/big sister. Finally, as gay rights groups began to insist that coming out was a necessary step in dissolving prejudice, and as Betty urged me to feel proud of my relationship with her, I gained the confidence to come out to my Mormon family. Mother cried, Dad put his arms around me and then around Betty, saying, "You're our daughter," he said to me, "You'll always be our daughter, and Betty will be, too." I loved him more at that moment than I could ever have imagined.

Even now, as I visit my parents, see the two of them leaving the clinic together after a family meeting, laughing and joking, telling old stories, I find it difficult to believe that my father is failing. His health is fine, his memory slightly impaired, but overall, he's in great shape. Hey, he's my Dad and he's going to be okay.

****

Nancy:

Dad never tried to draw *me* in, not his Nancy Ann. He always seemed to distrust me even as a small child. Perhaps it was because I was closer to Mom, looked more like her with my blonde hair and fair skin, and I think she sympathized with me, being a second child herself. So, I am daughter Number Two, the one who quarreled with Dad, sided with Mother, and always said what I thought.

I didn't have to perform the way my older sister did. By the time I was born, Marilyn had wowed the masses with her ability to memorize poems, sing, dance, think, and so on. I never had to impress anyone—I just watched as she got all the accolades. I didn't resent her because I felt people liked me just for who I was. I didn't need admiration.

Nearly three years separated us, so we were too far apart to be buddies. If my older sister tried to bully me, I fought back. Usually, we could find a tentative peace in which to share a room, toys and, sometimes, friends.

Mother wanted us, Marilyn and me, to be child stars, like Diana Durbin and Shirley Temple. Twice a week, she dressed us in outfits she had made herself and loaded us onto the street car for tap dancing and ballet lessons at The Meglin Studios, in Huntington Park. She was a stage mother, with dreams that her daughters would sing and dance their way to fame, letting the halo of their celebrity shine on her as she peeked out from the curtains. My sister hated me when I didn't remember the step sequence, but I didn't care because I could usually tap along, pretending to know the steps, all the while flashing a big smile to the audience. I grinned, while she bit her lip, trying to remember the steps. Yes, I watched, tried to adapt and always smiled at everyone.

Growing up in the suburb of Hollydale, California, I had no social consciousness, no sense of difference between people. Our neighborhood was mostly white, young families from places like Iowa and Michigan, whose parents had come to California during the War to find work in defense plants. They were like us, so how could I be prejudiced? But then there was

BROKEN CIRCUITS
A Memoir of Alzheimer's Disease in Four Voices

Dad. He was always spouting off about the Mexicans, how lazy they were, and I went to school with a lot of these kids. I wanted to get to know them, but I was afraid to ask them to my house. I don't know why he was so mean about them, but his stupid remarks always embarrassed me, especially when my friends were around.

Still, there are plenty of happy memories. On lazy summer afternoons, my friends and I would go down to the L.A. riverbed to look for doodle bugs, lizards and frogs, pairing up as "boyfriends" and "girlfriends" as we scavenged the area. It all just felt terribly normal. We played baseball in the street until our parents called us for dinner, then rushed to someone's family room to play Canasta. In 1953, when our neighbor Lou Reibsomer bought the first television in the neighborhood, I stood at her screen door without embarrassment, pressing my nose against the wire mesh to see the marvels of the modern age. My folks finally had to buy a TV set to keep me off from the neighbors front porch. Dad, ever the critic, called the set a "boob tube," but I never felt like a boob when I watched it. I felt like I had been set free. Now, I could not only watch my sister and her friends, my mom and dad, aunts and uncles and neighbors, but I could also watch kids from all over the country, discover how they talked, what their parents were like, how they treated each other. Little did I know, these sitcoms, like "I Love Lucy," would teach me to talk back to a bully of a father.

I learned quickly in school. My parents never worried about my grades or my performance, only that I talked too much. I was the lucky one, I guess, because I had many good friends. They were all Protestants or Catholics, and when they found out that I was a Mormon, they were curious, but really didn't care. For the most part, we didn't rebel or act out the way my own kids do today—smoking, drinking, testing the limits.

We were children of the fifties—naive, idealistic and ambitious. I was rarely sad, but when I was sad, it was usually because my friends had problems—or I had one with Dad. I was the "guardhouse lawyer" from the moment I hit puberty. I insisted on monitoring everyone's behavior, including Dad's, and telling them whenever they fell short. Once, when I was thirteen, he was talking about "his boy," how he and his son had to stick together against the women in the family. "You stupid fool!" I yelled at him, then careened through the front door, jumped off the front porch and fled down the sidewalk to escape his wrath. After a few hours at a friend's house, I came home, sneaked into my bedroom and hoped he had forgotten his anger. I learned to hit and run, not a great way to resolve differences, but at least I kept my integrity, even as a child.

My Dad and I took a long time to get through our mutual adolescence. I saw his contradictions and hypocrisies and he knew it. He thought he could shut me up the way he shut mother up—by intimidation. I wasn't going to be shut up, though. After years of combat, I left, went away to college, studied French, earned my teaching license and married my husband Lee. We've had seven children together. Sure, my Dad and I kept fighting, sometimes letting years go by hating each other, but by 1985, when we met at Bear Lake, we were getting along pretty well. I was doing fine and I thought that Dad was too, even though Mother reported on all the mistakes he was making—losing his checkbook, getting lost…a few accidents in the car. She loved to report this stuff and he was probably just teasing her. *Up to his old tricks,* I told myself after she called to

Mehr

tell me about the meeting at the Rancho. *He's probably just bored, playing a few games.*

****

<u>Judy:</u>

I'm the third daughter in a family of four children. My dad drew me in, all right. Why? I'll never know. Maybe it had something to do with roles: Marilyn, the performer; Nancy, the cut-up; and, Judy, the darling little coquette. My sister Marilyn was the doer, the planner, the "get things done-ster.". When Mom was weak, she leaned on Marilyn, asking her to organize the household and control the rest of us. But, both Mom and Dad confided in her, consulted about finances, travel, disputes with relatives, and even though she chose not to follow their religion, they respected her and her opinions, *always.*

Nancy and I were both middles, with three years between us, but she was more middle and I was treated more like the youngest. When I was two, my brother was born, and as Mom looked after the needs of the new baby Denny, I clung to my Daddy for love and nurturing. Looking back, I think he held me too closely. He used me for his own needs, for affection and admiration, and I gave it to him because I needed a place in this family. I learned to blink my big brown eyes at Dad and disarm his anger through childish flirtation. *Soothe the Tiger. Kiss him. Hug him. Make him be nice,* I learned. As I got older, I started to feel uncomfortable with all the petting and touching so I became hypercritical of everything he did. He took us to a church that preached that drinking alcohol was a sin, but there always a bottle or two under the sink and cold beer in the fridge in the summer. Whenever I challenged their hypocricy, they both laughed at me, and teased, "There goes Baby Judy in a temper."

When I was fourteen, I worried about their souls. It seemed to me that they were professing to be saints, but acting like sinners, so I asked Dad if he and mother would go to the new Los Angeles temple. Perhaps, I thought, the experience of solitude and prayer would transform them. They would return with an open heart, a determination to live by the church's guidelines about using alcohol and coffee, start taking care of themselves as true children of a loving God. Yes, I wanted them to be the perfect parents, my heroes in a world that I saw as pretty sinful.

Right away, Dad saw through my maneuverings and felt the judgment underneath my request. He pounded on the kitchen table, shouting that, "You can mind your own business, stop acting so goddamned holy, and leave me and your mother alone!" I was hurt, stunned and wounded. I began crying inconsolably. His response to my tears was to shout, "Stop it! Stop it right now or leave the room!!" I think he wanted to shake me or hit me, but he never did. He had no idea how to approach a kid who was becoming his own worst critic. As a parent, I know this is tough, but I've done it and know that my Dad could have reached me, if he had tried.

When each of us started to think for ourselves, we could see his hypocrisy, and Mom's too. Nance wrote him letters about "people who live in glass houses" and tried to show him that she, like Cordelia in King Lear, really loved him enough to criticize him. "Which of King Lear's daughters really loved him the most?" she would ask, eventually realizing that he had never read Shakespeare. Instead, he exploded. He had sent his daughters to college to give them the education he had missed, and now they were using it against him.

He loved us when we were little, his three darling girls, "Big Sissy," "Bootie," and "my little Snuggie Bunny" or more simply, "Snuggie," to Dad. We were not really close as children, but as adults, we've begun to discover our sisterhood. I'm like both of them, Marilyn and Nance. My sister, Nance, was blonde, Marilyn, a brunette and I had light brown curly locks. I also held the center between two extremes of social issues—Nancy was the traditional conservative upholding family and religious values, and Marilyn was ever the liberal, championing the rights of the poor and oppressed. I can see this same mixing of opposites in my third daughter, Heather, who is a similar blend of her two older sisters, Susan and Karin.

As I continued to grow up, I moved further away from my Dad and dated now and then, but my friends found me more brainy or "snobbish," than popular. I loved going to church and I loved my friends at church. In fact, I loved almost everything about it. And moderate that I was, I wanted to live my religion completely, not to follow Mother and Dad's lapses. I had a steady boyfriend my last year in high school and at the age of nineteen, I decided I would marry James Olson, the captain of the football team, the next summer, after I turned twenty. Mother was vehemently opposed to the marriage, not because she didn't admire Jim, but she just thought I was too young, sure to repeat the mistakes of her own marriage. She even offered to send him away on a church mission for two years to postpone the wedding!

We didn't ask our parents for permission or a blessing for our wedding. We would do as we wanted. Jim was young and ambitious, yet not really formed, but we grew up with each other and have loved one another for nearly thirty-two years. Eventually, both Mom and Dad became his greatest fans.

Dad really couldn't let go of me. Whenever he and Mom visited our home, he would sulk, refuse to leave the house, become rude with my friends. How do you talk about these things? "Dad, I think you're jealous that Jim and I are lovers. Want to talk about it?" Dad had his tantrums, while I went shopping with Mother and the kids.

Mom leaned on Marilyn and protected Nance from Dad's wrath, but she treated me like a little doll, not to be taken too seriously. When my oldest sister left for college, I stepped into her role as the pillar of strength, thinking that now I would at last be recognized as a person of substance. But even then, as the youngest of the three sisters, my parents never shared confidences with me. I longed for the very thing that Marilyn had resented—to be asked my opinion, to share a confidence or rely on me during tough time—to feel power within my own family. Funny, my oldest sister viewed herself as never fully respected because she didn't marry, nor did she follow her parents' religion. I did both of those things, and I never felt that I had gained their respect as an adult. *So how,* I now ask myself, *do you win at this game? How do you get them to see you as a strong, confident, capable adult?* I still don't know.

Between my marriage to Jim in '65 and the present, I grew up, mothered three wonderful daughters, Susan, Karin and Heather, and a very special son, Bradley. Over the years I have held positions of leadership within the Church, as has my husband. I get lonely sometimes when he goes away for his Church activities, particularly on the weekends. We have quarreled about his absence and then made up. At this point, we feel ever so close and happy to have each other. We have faced some very rough times together, the worst being the recurrence of a sarcoma which finally led to the amputation of his left arm in 1985. After living through those experiences, we have a different view of our lives, a sense of the tenuousness of our lives together and a need to be even closer.

Throughout this family is a subtext, as we say in my graduate school courses, a legacy bequeathed by our ancestors who joined a band of heretics in the Utah desert. Nancy and I have embraced the Mormon religion, while Marilyn and Denny have rejected it, preferring to find answers to questions of meaning in their own ways. Our decisions about the church have separated us, with two sisters on one side, a brother and sister on the other. I believe that Marilyn has grappled with her beliefs, but Den has avoided the subject, just disappearing when the subject is mentioned. Mother and Dad recognize this split, but have always been reluctant to confront it, preferring to love their children as they are and not run the risk of a major fracture.

So, at his moment, how are we doing? Marilyn and I are doing just fine. We've become sisters and friends, willing to trust and be sure of each other's loyalty. Nancy and I compete with one another, arguing about silly things, but we get over it. Dennis, my only brother and closest childhood friend, has never been willing to address or mend the gulf that grew when Jim and I married. I have often felt that I needed him, especially when Jim had cancer, and I wanted to be able to give to him, too, but I can't make it happen alone. My folks didn't teach us how to mend these ruptures, and I don't know how to do it alone. This is one of my life's deepest disappointments.

Still, my work is immensely rewarding. I teach immigrants, those without the language of their new country and those with major learning problems. Whether dyslexic or disinterested," they just can't read. And I'm determined to teach them. I went back to graduate school at the age of forty-two, in the midst of the crisis posed by the threat of my husband's cancer and the subsequent amputation of his arm. Jim insisted that I get my doctorate to "preserve your future earning power if I'm not around anymore." That's called "dying," isn't it? I could never really face losing him, but he made me realize that he might die, then he helped with all the work of juggling my job, my kids, my marriage, and my studies. He even typed drafts of my dissertation as a one-armed man! When I stood up to be hooded at graduation, in December of 1991, my husband and four children all cheered from their seats in the auditorium, "Yaaay, Mom!" I was so proud of myself, my children and my husband that I wanted to turn somersaults across the stage!

And now that Dad is slipping, I've got to deal with the family I thought I could leave behind: my two sisters, a Utah Mormon and an L.A. lesbian, and my brother, an Orange County partyboy! Jim insists that I can do this, that I'm strong, capable, achieving and loving—except in the presence of my family of origin. Perhaps I never really felt they were back there in the bleachers, cheering for me, so I looked toward the future, forged these tight bonds with my own kids. Susan, at twenty-eight, finds strength and fulfillment in teaching Mandarin Chinese; Karin, at twenty-six, loves practicing medicine in a small Texas town; and Heather, at twenty-four, has just finished her Master's degree and teaches high school Spanish. They are my daughters, my sisters, my friends. My son Brad has so many interests and talents that we can't know yet where his life will take him, but I know that being his mother has been and continues to be a special joy. There are now four more: Synneve, Elisa and Kennedy, and Colson, our grandkids. The future is so bright, but it's the past that carries a cloud. Everytime the phone rings and I hear Mother's voice, I know I've got to finish some business, left behind when I was twenty years old and married the nineteen year old guy who lived just over the railroad tracks.

****

Dennis:

Dad's illness made me think about my life, too. My sisters say they felt *drawn in* by Dad, but that never happened to me. No one drew *me* in. First of all, they could never find me. I was always gone somewhere, just "missing-in-action" during most of my childhood. I can't remember much of my childhood. Like my Dad, I have some "broken circuits," things I can't remember, people I've lost and have never found. I do remember that I always waited for him to come home at night. My friend, Joe Lucky, and I sat on the curb waiting, telling jokes, throwing rocks across empty fields, then as soon as we saw his truck, we'd run along the street, gaining enough speed to jump in the back for a free ride home.

Joe and I often played down by the riverbed, you know, Huck Finn/Tom Sawyer stuff—building forts, drifting through the rushes in our rafts. I never played in organized sports much, because the church had its own recreational programs and didn't encourage you to join the "outsiders." 'Sounds a little paranoid, I guess, and it was. You know, never trust the non-believers! Look out for Satan! All that stuff. That's all I remember, though, waiting for the truck and rafting the L.A. River, at least until I was about fifteen or sixteen. I never felt like anyone really knew what I was doing. Now I don't know whether they do, either.

When I got a driver's license at sixteen, that was my ticket out. Mother was back in school and everybody else was gone, so I never stayed home. Judy tried to keep track of me, but I was always out of touch. Three sisters who were little stars in the sky of Paramount High School and a brother who was Halley's comet! In high school, when I really screwed up, the vice-principal, Mr. Roselle, called me the "black sheep" of the family because my GPA was on the skids. If he could see the slope I was on, why couldn't my Dad? He didn't have to look at my grades, he could have seen that I was suspended for fighting, not once, but several times. In my senior year I missed almost 40 days of school. Sure, I forged notes so no one knew, but they could have looked at the absences on the report card. It got even worse. In two years, when I was sixteen and seventeen, I wrecked four cars! In fact, I wrecked Dad's Ford truck the night before Nancy's wedding and I called him from a pay phone beside Pacific Coast Highway to tell him the news. He went stone silent, then just muttered in this deep, dead voice, "Don't bother to come home, you little bastard!" What did I care? I knew he'd change his mind. In the meantime, I thought I had wings and could fly.

I was a teenager and starting to see all of the hypocricy in the Mormon church, as well as in my parents. They were nice to everybody on Sunday, then spent the rest of the week criticizing them. There was good reason. The so-called "elders" acted like they had a direct line to God and were bent out of shape because I questioned them. It wasn't their story about Joe Smith and baptising the dead people that turned me off, it was a lot of people messing with me. Just one example. Kelly Hickman beat up that dumb kid, named Crossley, and the elders told Kelly he was going to burn in hell, that he was a blight on his own family and so on. Kelly was my friend and they treated him like a serial killer. From then on, I went to church with Mom and Dad, but I would find Kelly, walk right through the chapel and across the parking lot to the liquor store where we bought candy bars and waited until the meeting was over. I passed right through those holy doorways for a lot of years until finally, I just quit.

I knew what I was doing. I knew right from wrong, okay, but I didn't care what happened. Dad never noticed what was happening, or at least, he never said anything about all my screw-ups, except for the time I wrecked his truck and then he never spoke about it again. I wasn't acknowledged much by anyone. I was just *The little brother who just came and went.* There was no input from my folks, no limits. I wanted someone to stop me, but no one did.

When I was younger, I wanted Dad's company, but whenever I would suggest that we go somewhere together, his favorite retort was, "I never lost anything there. Why bother?" There were two times that he gave in. Once, when I was ten and had made a go-cart scooter, he took Kelly Hickman and me out to the desert to ride around and shoot guns. I have no idea where he got the 22 rifles, but he took us. Then, about 1961, when I was fourteen, he took Kelly and me fishing at Crenshaw

Lake. Mother probably made him take us because he really didn't seem to be having much fun. The first night, we slept in the truck at a rest stop. In the morning, he bought us breakfast, then took us fishing. Nobody caught a thing, so we went to a trout farm and caught a few fish which we showed to mother as proof of a successful father/son outing. I really didn't have any fun, either.

The second time we went away together, Dad took me and another friend to Oceanside where we slept in a market parking lot in the back of a camper. I'll never know why he thought we should sleep in parking lots. It may be that he couldn't figure out how to find an R.V. park, so he just pulled up into a Safeway's, turned out the lights and went to sleep. It was eerie sleeping in those places, people driving in and out all night. Again, we got up real early and fished off the pier for a few hours and went home. I knew he didn't want to do these trips. He just didn't try very hard to make it fun.

What he liked to do was work and ridicule people. All through the fifties, he would come home after a long week, sit down and take his shoes off on the front porch, belittle the neighbors and tease his kids. Maybe this behavior covered his insecurity, but I hated it. When I was nineteen, I was glad to enlist in the service as soon as I got the chance. There was no one home, I was walking the edge, and I wanted out. Who cared about Vietnam?

I didn't care about Vietnam, although I never got there. I spent four years in Arizona, at Lackland Air Force Base and when I got out, I felt whole for the first time in my life. They had given me a lot of responsibility as a dispatcher. I controlled the scheduling, man hours, materials, and I did a damned good job. Then, my tour of service was up and I came home to Los Angeles and joined my Dad's business. One of the first days I worked with him, I expressed some political opinions, about the war, I guess, and he told me I was wrong, stupid, uninformed. I broke down and cried. I was twenty-two years old and just starting to feel some pride in myself. That was the last time we talked about anything real—1970. He made me feel empty and small. He won, but I never forgot it.

Stay out of the way—that's how I learned to get along with him. I did a good job, not because it was expected of me, but because there was only his way. I just lay low, kept myself camouflaged, because you never knew when he would blow.

His fits were irrational. He would walk into the shop smiling, one of the employees would take a few minutes too long to answer the phone, and Dad would explode. No one had to be the cause of these eruptions, but any one of us could sure could be the result.

Why didn't I leave? Oh, I don't know. When I returned from the Air Force, I enrolled in school, but I had an unplanned child—not an excuse, just and event—and Dad provided a house for Linda and me as part of our "contract." It was easy, if you didn't mind his fits. I saved a lot of money, enough to buy a three-bedroom house in a nearby suburb, called Cerritos, even though he didn't pay me a lot. At first, I enjoyed school, but the kids in college seemed kind of young and naive. I wasn't that much older than the others, but I was more mature. I didn't fit. Or they didn't fit. I liked literature and movie classes and am still a film buff. Dad never understood or cared about my interests. If we talked, it was always about the business or some odd-ball customer, like Arnie, the Arkansan, who always wanted to sell us moonshine whiskey.

In ten years, I had a new house, two condos in Mammoth, a sailboat, two kids and was having a hell of a time.

Mehr

Who had time for school? I just forgot about it. I was careful with my money, but I could still afford our weekends in Mammoth and ski passes for the kids. Life was pretty good. Then, I started looking for land to build some houses. I had this dream of being a big-time contractor. Suddenly, the economy went bust, I lost $70,000.00 in one day and a little switch went off in my heart.

You know, it never occurred to me to ask my Dad for help. I haven't ever and I couldn't. He never knew what I was doing and if he had lent me money, he would have known if I failed. He never knew what I did in the service, either. He never even asked. That was all for me.

My life took a stall about that time. It was 1980. I had gotten beaten up in a land deal and I just laid down for awhile and didn't get up again for a long time. Sure, I went to work, but I was like a zombie, with big hollow eyes, staring out at the world and not feeling. Yes, I started to drink a lot. Sadly enough, I wasn't all there.

In a few days, it will be Thanksgiving, 1985. I'm still not all here. Maybe I'll face up to my past one day, but in the meantime, I have to figure out how to help this guy who sits and stares from his little office beside the shop. I love him and hate him. Which side is going to win?

***

CHAPTER FIVE

A GOLDEN ANNIVERSARY (1936-1986)

> 12/2/85
>
> <u>Psychological Assessment:</u> Pt. is a 75-y.o. Caucasian male who is being evaluated to determine his degree of memory impairment as well as any concomitant psychological issues. He displayed a depressed affect and minimal eye contact. His attention varied and he would mutter and complain at times. His wife stated that he had complained bitterly about the exam beforehand.
>
> <u>Summary:</u> This pt. demonstrated strengths in naming, availability of general information and a sense of time. His attention to details, effort and concentration were poor and he needed repeated cueing. He was particularly impaired in motor coordination tasks, becoming extremely frustrated in his attempts. His expressive abilities are poor, given his fund of information. Although he reports no depression on paper and pencil measures he presents some vegetative signs.

> Impressions:
> 1. Mild memory impairment, probably consistent with early stages of Alzheimer's.
> 2. Mild depression secondary to above.
>   (signature) Alex Kelly, Ph.D., Gero Service

<u>Marilyn:</u>

If our experience at Bear Lake taught us anything, it underscored for my sisters and me the importance of holding family gatherings while Dad could still enjoy them. We had the opportunity of celebrating a significant anniversary for our parents, fifty years of marriage, on January 3, 1986. Mother was hesitant to plan a party. She was becoming ever more cautious about Dad's ability to socialize and even her own. We urged her to allow us to start planning.

Instead, she smiled and told us about their wedding. "We were married on a cold winter day, January 3, 1936, in the Logan Temple. I hadn't been sure that I wanted to get married, but Dad's brother, Otto, drove up to our family home in his new Stutz Bearcat, talked to my parents, Roy and Marcia and tried to persuade them to let me marry Al. He painted this rosy picture of your Dad becoming the Operations Manager for the new business in Dayton, having all these opportunities to grow and make a good salary. Don't forget, it as the middle of the Depression. Then, came the punchline. He tells them that Dad would never make it without Vivian. They looked at me to see my reaction. I smiled and they said *yes.*"

"What about your dreams of going back to school, Mom?" Judy had asked. As a woman struggling to finish graduate school, Judy understood the many conflicts between family and professional ambitions. She listened intently as Mother spoke.

"I was reluctant to give up my dreams of a college education, but I was excited about being able to travel. I had never been anywhere farther away than Salt Lake and neither had any of my friends. I wanted to see more of the world and I couldn't see how I could ever finish school."

"Didn't you have doubts about whether Dad was ready to get married?" This time I asked the question, having heard stories about his reputation as a roustabout in Cache Valley.

"Yes, I thought about that. Your Dad liked to drink and smoke, drive the ladies around in his Model-A coupe. He never seemed able to get up on Sunday mornings to attend church. I knew he could never get the Bishop's permission, a *recommend,* for a wedding in the temple."

"So, how did he get one?" Nancy asked, curious about how he could bend church rules. She believed in living by the letter of the law and was annoyed when others manipulated church doctrine.

"Well, he kept bothering me, so I challenged him and said, 'You can't get a recommend. You smoke and drink, and can't get up on Sunday morning to go to church. The Bishop will never give *you* a recommend."

She enjoyed telling this story, relishing her provocation. "He knew full well that a *recommend* was supposed to be a declaration from his ward Bishop that verified the good conduct of its recipient. It confirmed that the holder had attended church services regularly, abstained from alcohol and tobacco, and was sexually chaste. Without this declaration, no one can participate in any of the ceremonies held in a Mormon temple. Your Dad complied with none of these rules, but he came back with a handful of them." In the arrogance born of youth and desire, he believed that the Bishop could be persuaded of his intent to reform. After all, his parents had long ago purchased a place in this community of Saints by sacrifice and devotion, years of labor on the eastern plains of Utah. Their son was entitled to some of its benefits of their good standing. The twenty-five year old son of Swiss immigrants kissed his girlfriend goodbye and drove directly to the home of his Bishop where he presented his case.

By nightfall, he returned with *recommends* for himself, his future wife, her parents and his own parents who now lived in Logan. Perhaps it was his determination that persuaded Mother, or just his brashness. Throughout their lives together, she always admired his challenge of authority, even though she feigned embarrassment at his audacity. Despite her conventional demeanor, she shared with her husband a deep distrust for those in power—government officials, even church authorities—a suspicion passed on to each of their four children.

At our family reunion at Bear Lake, Mother admitted she was superstitious about holding a celebration of their anniversary. She worried that celebrating longevity of life, relationships, commitment, represented a form of hubris. By marking the passage of time, one called attention to the gods that life was a bit too bright, that some tempering would no doubt follow, righting the balance of darkness with light. Mother never delved very deeply into these feelings, preferring to laugh and say, "Let's not tempt fortune."

"Don't forget, Mom. You've taken quite a few risks before," I argued, "and things turned out okay. Didn't you go back to school at forty? Didn't you charge off on a cold January morning in the middle of the Depression to a place fifteen hundred miles from home? You can surely have a party without provoking a calamity."

She agreed, but she seemed to lack enthusiasm. Taking care of Dad was exacting a price. Her attention was focused on his every move, noting his location, monitoring his eating and sleeping. She also worried about Dad's ability to meet and greet so many friends in a pressured situation. "Will he be able to remember their names? Will he tire under the strain?"

We reassured her that we would all watch out for Dad, supply him with names of old friends, find him a chair if he tired. She still wasn't certain, wanting more time to consider "whether it's going to be worth all that effort."

BROKEN CIRCUITS
A Memoir of Alzheimer's Disease in Four Voices

In early September, I called my brother and asked him to help me encourage our parents to make a decision about their anniversary party. We met them at a favorite Mexican restaurant in East Los Angeles, surrounded by waterfalls, miniature lakes and palm trees. Dennis and I reassured them that fifty years of marriage was well worth celebrating and that we would all make it a warm and happy occasion. My brother then suggested renting a party room at a local restaurant or hotel. In fact, we had both brought brochures from caterers, with photographs of buffet tables as well as cost estimates. To our surprise, Mother and Dad had already decided to go ahead with the reception. They preferred the familiarity of the large recreational room in their local chapel in Downey, and had spoken to a local church member about catering. Dennis and I gave each other high five's and said that we would hire a band. The party was on.

Mother seemed pleased and participated in plans for the event. However, as usual, she masked her worries about Dad with endless stories and titters. One day in November, I came home from work to find a letter from her in my mailbox. It seemed strange that she would write to since we only lived

Mehr

twenty-five miles apart, but she had. I went into the house, changed clothes, made a cup of tea and opened the envelope.

November 5, 1985

Dear Marilyn,

'Thought I'd write this note to you while I have a few minutes to myself. There's so *damned* much "have to" stuff every *day* that I stay up half the *night* just to have time to do for myself. When I write my book it'll be called,

"I HAVE TO…"

Resentment builds up and I get angry too easily.

This morning I wrote two checks—put in envelopes and addressed them—Started to look for stamps—By the time I found them (after a few interruptions) I'd lost the 2 envelopes—After much frustration I found them in the bottom of the wastebasket with some other stuff. I hurried and stamped them and walked down to the mailbox!

I hope the rest of the day goes better. I have an appointment for a massage tomorrow a.m. I feel as tho' my blood pressure is up. Maybe the massage will help.

'Guess I'll list what I have to do and get started crossing them off instead of worrying.

I spent yesterday housecleaning my bedroom because I awoke feeling something inside my ear—*moving*! I got a hairpin and cleaned it out and it was an ant deep inside my ear—Then I looked around the base board and saw some others, so I deep-cleaned and sprayed around the outside and inside. I hope that takes care of it but if we go away to our condo, a batch of *fleas* and *ants* will probably be in the house! You've heard of bats in the *belfry*???

They did that scan on Dad's head Tuesday and we see the pictures Thursday. Perhaps you can find a time for Dr. Chin to show them to you, just for your own information. We'll see...

I'd better get going—

Love, Mom

P. S. I'm making two lists for the anniversary invitations: "classy" friends, those with flowers for the artistic; "non-classy," the others for the autistic...

Mehr

I dropped the letter on the table and began to cry. My mother was not only tired, she was becoming *peculiar*. If I couldn't persuade her that she needed some help, she was going to get worse, more depressed, less capable of taking care of Dad or herself. I decided to call a friend who was a social worker, get some information on home assistants and then call my sisters and brother. I was beginning to feel like a social worker myself, but not a very good one.

Despite Mother's frustrations over the increasing pressures of caring for a husband who was becoming increasingly impaired, she sent the invitations and nearly two hundred and fifty people showed up at the reception on January 3rd. Both Dad and Mother stood at the head of the line greeting friends they had known for almost a lifetime. If Dad forgot some of their names, he remembered faces and covered his lapses with an affectionate hug, a big smile and his gratitude for their company.

Few people recognized that Dad was not entirely himself and few people realized how hard Mother was trying to present a family that was happy and whole. On the surface, we looked fine, all dressed up in party clothes, smiling for the camera. Nonetheless, the truth was that her husband had lost most of his memory, her oldest daughter had brought a female lover and her two other daughters still held deep and simmering resentments towards parents they still called "hypocrites."

The months preceding the anniversary party had been laced with fierce accusations and petty insults, as we four children each re-played old dramas of childhood. My sister Judy attempted to heal a rift with my brother that had existed since her marriage with Jim. Whenever she tried to call Dennis, he once again rejected her, saying he was "too busy" to talk. She wanted to talk and he didn't and she was left feeling hurt and mystified. "Why won't he talk to me?" she would ask her sisters. We couldn't answer, but urged her to come to the anniversary party for Mother and Dad. "Forget about your brother for now," we advised.

Nancy, on the other hand, recalled all of Dad's blaming and criticism of her throughout her childhood. She remembered, but didn't want to talk to him about her feelings. The more incidents she remembered, the harder it became to keep quiet. I thought he was still able to listen and understand some of her resentments, but she didn't trust him. "It's easy for you to say," she told me. "You psychologists think there's an answer for everything."

No, I didn't, and as the gay "member of the wedding," I worried about how Betty and I should present ourselves, how visible we should be in showing our love for each other. The choice to attend a public ceremony as an out gay couple might seem simple to those who were born after the many civil rights revolutions beginning in the sixties. Yet, Betty and I had come of age during the Eisenhower years when women were expected to marry, give up their jobs and devote themselves to their families. They were not expected to love other women and have exciting careers. At times, we still hid our relationship, even though we were both members of gay rights groups, had worked actively to pass Proposition Six, the anti-gay initiative, and were out to most of our friends. In spite of our progress, we weren't ready to dance at the fiftieth wedding reception of my Mormon parents.

Ours was not "the love that had no name." Everyone in the immediate family knew we were a couple, and tried, whenever Betty would agree, to include us in family dinners and events. As an only child, Betty had little experience with the give and take of family life and usually preferred her own company. She also believed that as Mormons my family really saw her as sinful and even when they embraced her, they were just being hypocrites. I had given up inviting her to most family events, but I wanted her to attend my parents' fiftieth wedding anniversary. We were two bright, attractive and accomplished women who had every reason to be proud of our place in this family. I wanted her to be there at my side.

We were still concerned about how my parents felt about our presence as a couple. Of course, we had talked to them years earlier about ourselves and tried to share the importance and richness of our relationship. After that, everyone seemed to forget about the subject, never referring to the conversation, but nonetheless, trying to include Betty in family events. I was sure that neither of my parents had told their family or friends about us, although I knew that families always knew one another's "secrets." The anniversary would force some decisions. What was Betty's role in the family? Would she stand beside me in the reception line? Would she appear in all of the family photographs? Would we dance

Mehr

together when the band started to play? *How public would we be?*

After endless discussions about both the personal and political significance of our coming out, we decided to let our parents decide. If it were our party, we would be out and open. Since it was their anniversary, we would do whatever made them feel comfortable.

I waited until the night before the reception, the second of January, to talk with them. Finally, when just my parents and two sisters were left at the dinner table, I opened the discussion with my parents.

"You know, Mom and Dad, we haven't talked about what you want tomorrow night, you know, as far as Betty and I are concerned." I hesitated for a minute, hoping my sisters would help me if I needed it. "And, uh, in particular, what about the reception line and the family photos? What do you want Betty and me to do?"

Mother looked out the front window at a passing car while Dad looked puzzled. Does he understand my question, I wondered. He scratched his head for a moment, then smiled and squeezed my hand.

"Sure I want Betty to be there, the whole thing." he said as though there couldn't be any question. I smiled back, loving him for his simple trust and generosity.

Then, the doorbell rang. As he got up to answer it, my Mother whispered to me covertly, "But not in the reception line."

I was stunned, hurt and angered by her sneakiness, but unable to respond in the presence of a group of friends and family now entering through the front door. An agreement was an agreement, I told myself, and prepared to leave. Betty and I would live with Mother's decision, rather than protest. When I told Betty later, the story confirmed her expectations.

"I thought so," she said, "but I said I would go and I will."

The reception was a huge success on many levels. There were people who appeared from every corner of my parents' lives. I stood in the line for awhile, then sat with Betty and her parents at one of the tables surrounding the dance floor. Some of our friends have encouraged us to credit my parents for overcoming their religious beliefs and including both of us as family. I believe they love me, but I also believe that my mother could have extended her love to Betty. She fell short of my expectations and so did I. My place should have been at the table with Betty, not in the receiving line with my family. Until they can acknowledge her as my partner, my place is beside her, whether at the table or in the parking lot carrying a banner for gay pride. I had made a mistake which I will never repeat again.

I also realized that my mother was frightened of what others might think of her, and that, typically, my father didn't give a damn. He loved his family first and everyone else would always be far behind. I knew I was losing that fierce devotion. I could still see the light burning in his eyes when he realized what I had asked. "The whole thing," he had said and meant it.

****

<u>Judy:</u>

As one of the supposedly "good" daughters, one who married, went to Texas, had four kids and stayed in the Mormon church, I wasn't looking forward to this "golden" reception. Mother had called me several times. "Judy, I don't think he can handle this," and I reassured her that he could. Yet, we were all tense and worried that Dad might not be capable of handling a three or four hour evening of friends, family, food and music. Fortunately, my parents preferred their old Downey Second Ward recreation room as the site, basketball hoops and all. In fact, Dad had helped to build that church nearly twenty-five years before.

Then there was the "problem" of Marilyn and Betty. I wasn't worried, but as soon as I arrived on the 30th of December, Mom started fretting about what people were going to think about the two of them. Marilyn had been honest with all of us and we all knew that this was a gay relationship, but Mother hadn't been open with any of her friends or family. Finally, when she saw the list of names for the florist, which naturally included Betty's, she questioned me. "Do you think you should?" she asks, without really revealing her own discomfort.

I said, "Oh, yeah, sure," and ordered the flowers. There was no doubt in my mind that Betty was part of our family whether she wanted to be or not. But, simply offering Betty a corsage forced Mother to realize that her family and friends might discover one of our family secrets! Just to make matters worse, my brother's wife, Linda, had a few drinks and called Marilyn to tell her that all of us were going to the temple to pray for Marilyn and Betty's souls! Believe me, it never happened. Yes, we went to the temple and yes, we prayed, but for ourselves, not for a change in two people's sexual orientation! We went to the temple on the 2nd of January so that Mom and Dad could renew their vows, the same vows they had taken in the Logan Temple in 1936. I hoped their promises both to love *and* respect each other might stick this time. After fifty years, perhaps they could learn to love each other. Everyone in the family seemed to getting a little nutty around this anniversary celebration and I thought a visit to the temple might at least bring some temporary peace. If not, and I wanted to go home. To hell with all of them!

As I watched Dad walk beside Mother through the silent white halls of the temple, I would think about Dad, fading away into his own foggy world. He had bought Mom some beautiful diamond-studded earrings. but he never took part in any of the discussions about flowers or photographs or receiving lines. He was present, but not attentive. His affableness seemed strange, so out of character.

I also began to see my mother in a different light, as someone who was honest about the superficialities of life, but not the nitty gritty of telling others the truth. I've tried to be honest with my own children, because I think we can love each other when we're not pretending. Of course, sometimes I've hurt them, and I guess that's why Mother avoided telling us the truth. She wanted everything painful to be erased so that everyone could be happy, whatever that was. My mother couldn't cope very well with reality.

****

Nancy:

I arrived the same day as my sister Judy and wasn't nearly as troubled by the undercurrent of strife. Perhaps, I'm used to it as a mother of seven children. Perhaps, I've just learned to ignore it. Anyhow, I enjoyed the anniversary celebration tremendously—all the old friends, the gathering of family. In fact, my husband Lee was having such a good time dancing that he said to me, "Nance, let's stay a few extra days. I'm sure the kids would love it and so would their grandparents." I was hesitant because I knew that Christmas had always been a rough time at our house on Pennsylvania Avenue. Dad always became so moody and unpredictable when we were kids that I didn't want to stress him, particularly around my own kids. Let them have their memories of a nice, kindly old man who took them to the dime store and passed out dollar bills for shopping.

It was too easy to recall my own memories of Christmas. If Mother played the piano while her children sang Christmas carols, he would feel left out because he couldn't sing well and if he did try, someone might make a joke about his atonal humming. Mom was the star of our musical world and had taught her children to love music. We would encircle her on the piano bench, singing in chorus, until she finally ended the session belting out, "Put Your Arms Around Me, Honey, Hold Me Tight!" as she bounced in rhythm and we all giggled.

My memories of Dad fighting and sulking were less painful this holiday, especially with all the good feelings now surrounding the golden anniversary party. Yet, I still felt an underlying tenseness, especially when I let myself remember the Christmas from Hell. It had been so shattering for all of us that I usually tried to forget the whole experience.

BROKEN CIRCUITS
A Memoir of Alzheimer's Disease in Four Voices

What happened? It's hard to recall even now, but I remember that I was nearly sixteen years old and even had my own car, a 1950 Chevy. Dad bought each of us a used car when we got our licenses and even though we expressed our appreciation, he always felt that we took him for granted. "All you kids want is my money," he would yell in exasperation as the price of Christmas grew. We did love him and tried to show it, but we couldn't have known that he was fighting his own painful memories of growing up on the plains with only three apples for dinner. We just knew that in the middle of the happiest occasions, Santa Claus might explode.

On Christmas Day, 1958. Mom invited one of her bosses from the local funeral parlor, Dave Chandler, and his wife for refreshments and a holiday chat. I was supposed to be in the kitchen doing dishes, but the sun was shining and at fourteen, I found it hard to stay indoors. Talking to a friend over the back fence, I suddenly heard Dad yelling that I should get into the house and finish "the damn dishes!" I said, "Why don't you do them yourself?" just to show off to my friend and he lunged at me, grabbing my arm and dragging me across the back yard to the kitchen door, screaming.

Just as we reached the steps, I coughed. He must have thought I was laughing at him because he grabbed my collar and kneed me in the tail bone until I fairly flew over the transom. Then, my mother appeared and started shouting, too.

"Leave her alone, Al. We've got company!"

"You think you and your goddamned friends are so smart!" he yelled at her.

She stood in the doorway, humiliated and enraged, "Well, they've got more couth than you, you stupid jackass!"

Of course, the guests were so embarrassed that they left immediately, leaving Mom embarrassed and torn between her daughter and husband. This scene—Mother and Dad fighting, hurling insults over my head—was repeated in different ways in my childhood endlessly.

As I look back on the whole sad affair, I know my smart remarks weren't all that bad. If Dad were really honest, he might have admitted that he was jealous of the guy in the living room who had driven up in a new Buick Roadmaster and was sitting on his couch smoking Havana stogies, telling stories that made his wife and our mother roar with laughter. Was I just a player in the theater of Dad's Inferiority Complex?

I'll never know, but I know I've had back problems ever since our battle and an emotional scar that's even worse.

So, I thought. The Christmas Day fight was thirty years ago. We've all changed, grown up some, and the dramas of the past don't have to replay themselves. I was wrong. Once more, the conflict erupted between me and Dad. It seemed so, because this awful drama played out one more time in the family living room with all of Mom's living siblings and spouses as witnesses. Yes, Dad was stressed by having eleven of his thirteen grandchildren staying at the house surrounded by all of Mom's family. So was I and so was everyone, but we were getting along, until my son Peter set off the *I Hate Christmas* reprise. There they were, Peter and his friend Eric, working on their car when Dad walked up and asked what they were doing. Peter said they were having trouble fixing the starter. Dad couldn't wait to charge into the house and tell everyone how stupid my son was and how lame-brained his friend was. I responded like a mother tiger protecting her young.

This time I was *doing* the damned dishes when I heard his tirade. All of the other visitors were with Mother in the living room where Dave and his wife had sat thirty years ago. I began sotto voce, calmly disagreeing with him, saying that, "Peter is really a smart kid, Dad, but he doesn't know much about cars yet."

Then he pushed the envelope, as they say, insisting that, "Your son is just a lazy bum! Pete hasn't got an ounce of ambition in him. He'll never amount to a hill of beans!"

The veins in my head began to throb, and I spat the words out at him, "You know, you're just plain crazy! You're off your stupid gourd!"

He blocked the doorway, his face red with anger. "Don't you ever talk to me that way!"

I planted my feet at the sink. This was war. "I'll say whatever I want. I'm that kid's mother! You can try to ruin my life, you stupid fool, but you're not ruining my kid's!"

All of a sudden Mother appeared and begins patting his shoulder. I couldn't believe my eyes! She was sticking up for this cruel brute. *How could she?*

I'd had enough of this family madness so I took off with my mother's youngest brother, Royal, who tried to tell me that my father wasn't himself, that the Alzheimer's made it hard to control his outbursts. *Not himself?* He was only too much himself. That was the funniest thing anyone had said in a day of very funny outbursts. I began laughing until I crumpled over on the curb where I finally let myself cry. Through it all, I told my uncle a few things he may not have known, such as what it was like to grow up with a child-man instead of a father and just how good it felt to finally tell him off. I may have felt some tenderness at the lake, but now I felt a pure molten fury. Uncle Royal sat beside me on the curb, listened, blinked and swallowed, waited until my rage dissolved into tears, then finally put his arms around me, a big loving hulk of a guy who knew what to do.

Lee and I knew what to do, too. We immediately gathered our children together and left. Pete and Eric suddenly figured out how to start their car and they left, too. I was mad for about three hundred miles and then, stupidly, I began to feel guilty because I believed my explosion would contribute to Dad's confusion and decline. I even imagined that the stress of our fighting caused him to have a small stroke later that month. Even though I knew I hadn't harmed him, I still tried to soften my anger, making it up to him in small ways, sending him funny cards, and returning the next year for more frequent visits. We never talked about the anniversary tornado and, as Dad predicted, my son Pete went on to ruin his life, never fixing the starter that would drive him away from self-destruction and shame. I feel guilty about that, too, even though Lee and I have deeply searched our actions to try to learn what we could have done to keep him from becoming an addict. Will my son ever *amount to anything?* We'll see. One thing I know, that I'll always feel proud that I refused to let his grandfather call him "stupid!"

On our way to Sacramento where we were visiting some old friends, I thought about my parents, getting more perspective as the miles passed. They were both very intelligent, but they lacked "people skills." Mom went through the motions of tact and politeness in public—especially with those who were outside of the family. People always thought she was serene, sweet, kind and gentle, but, she was sometimes mean and petty, especially with Dad. Now that he was getting weaker, she was finally retaliating for all his slights and insults, acting like a nineteen-year old bearing fifty years of grudges. They blurted out whatever they feel regardless of the damage to their children. I hate to admit it, but I've done that too, exploded on my children, and I wish I could have stopped myself.

It's easy to do, letting go. I've said, "Oh, the hell with it, I'm going to say this anyway." My worst outburst occurred several years ago when my husband Lee went away with a friend of his, supposedly to sell insurance, although I wasn't sure whether he wasn't really just escaping from me and our seven kids. As the evening wore on, I started to imagine he was leaving us, that I would be left alone in this little California suburb with all our kids to raise. In the middle of my worries, one of the older ones let our middle daughter, Carrie, slip in the bathtub. I ran into the bathroom, picked her up and started screaming at all the children.

"Why didn't you watch her? What's wrong with you? All you do is take, take, take...never think of anyone but yourselves!" I just screamed and screamed and screamed until the neighbors called the police. Two guys in blue showed up at the door, looked through the screen and said, "Is something wrong here?" They must have thought my children were being killed.

I suddenly returned to sanity, realizing how I had just vented all these horrible feelings on my children. They had been wounded badly and I had been unable to stop myself. I didn't hit them, but I just kept yelling. They had to be terrified and I had provoked that terror. The demons inside me had won, just as they had with my father. All of my insecurity and fear were turned against my own children and I was so ashamed.

I finally said to the cops, "I'm fine. I just don't know where my husband is. He was supposed to be home by ten." They looked around, checked for bruises, seemed satisfied that I was in control and left. The whole nightmare was very embarrassing and sad. It was my fault, but Lee must share some of the blame. These were his children and he had run away, if only for an evening. I couldn't. I had a brand new baby and I snapped.

I did a lot of thinking as we traveled up Highway Five after the anniversary party. This road is endless, a long straight stretch through the central California plains, so I had plenty of time to review all that had happened, particularly in the dark with the kids asleep in the back of the van. Yes, Dad had snapped, too, and it wasn't completely his fault. He had been raised by a father who was very intolerant, not warm or loving, and who probably blew up when he was angry. So what did Dad learn? You either beat your kid or blew up. "Get out of here, you damn fool!" Dad had been told. He learned some awful lessons from his father which he passed on to me. The difference between us is that I'm sorry and I've apologized to my children and he hasn't.

My father could have vented his rage on my brother and sisters, but I'm convinced that he targeted me because I never could keep my mouth shut. If I had an opinion, I expressed it, or if he treated Mother unfairly, I had to defend her. He called me "Mother's guardhouse lawyer," and I guess I was. I tried to defend Mother because she wouldn't defend herself. She would try, but always gave up and cried. I hated to see her that way and would always speak up. It seemed a grave injustice to let him win.

****

Mehr

<u>Dennis:</u>

Some people called this a "golden" anniversary, but their son wasn't one of them. My parents have been married for a long time, but it hasn't been a happy time, most of it. I showed up for the party, anyway, and wore a flower in my buttonhole. I smiled a lot, made a big display of old photographs that everybody liked, but I wasn't really there. I was somewhere else, inside my own head, thinking to myself that I didn't ever want to repeat their lives. I didn't want to repeat any of their lives—grandparents, aunts and uncles. I don't have to and I won't.

***

CHAPTER SIX

PROTECTING OUR OWN—1987-88

> 8/19/87 Family Conference with pt. and wife, Vivian, daughter and son-in-law, Jim and Judy Olson, and daughter, Marilyn Mehr
>
> Diagnosis: Amnestic Syndrome
>   hypertension
>   hearing loss
>   adjustment reaction to retirement
>
> Subjective: Long discussion—Pt. felt he was being "demeaned." At first felt he said he didn't have any problems. Slipped quickly into denial when memory issues were directly attacked. Very upset about retirement and "worthlessness." Doesn't feel useful. Not working much at auto parts store, not involved in church activities as he has had a falling out with the Bishop.

> Plan: Jim, his son-in-law, will talk with the Bishop about it. Al agreed to come regularly (q. 2 wks) for counseling with me and get hearing eval. I will see him privately without his wife or residents.
>
> (signature) K. Brummel-Smith, M.D.

Marilyn:

The "golden" anniversary hadn't been an unqualified success, but it brought many of Mother and Dad's friends into one room to celebrate their years of knowing one another, working together as church members and sharing their joys as parents. The party had also healed a few rifts in our family, but exposed others that were still raw. I suppose that's as much as one can expect from any single event and, for me, it was good enough.

When Judy and Jim arrived for a visit in July of the following year, I asked them to attend a family meeting at The Rancho where they could meet Dad's doctor, hear his evaluation and contribute to some support to those of us who were living in California, my brother and me, and were Mother's primary resource. We were doing well, a mother and her children, and believed we could offer whatever was necessary to allow Dad to remain in his home with mother. After all, we were all healthy, our spouses and partners were fine. Fate had blessed us and there was no reason to expect that our lives would become any more difficult.

Unexpectedly, all of our family planets were hit by a meteor. In the year following the anniversary, each of our spouses or partners experienced a major threat to their health. We tried to pay attention to our father's needs, as well as our mother's fatigue, but we couldn't begin to handle two serious illnesses at once. Judy experienced the first crisis.

****

<u>Judy:</u>

Even though Marilyn had told me about the Older Adult Center at the Rancho, I wasn't prepared for the kindness and attention that was offered to us when we attended the family meeting with Dad. His doctor as well as the staff really seemed to want to help all of us to cope with Dad's illness. Jim and I were eager to do whatever we could. We would call Dad's Bishop and emphasize Mother's need for help. Surely, he would respond. Mother and Dad had both given so much to the church throughout their lives—money, time, sweat equity—that they were entitled now to receive something in return.

What neither Jim nor I had foreseen was the dark shadow hovering over our own family. Two weeks after we returned to our home in Texas, the sarcoma on Jim's wrist reappeared. A team of doctors at M.D. Anderson examined him and they all recommend amputation, just below the elbow. We had known this could happen, having faced a long series of radiation treatments for the sarcoma six years earlier, followed by another series of surgeries to remove small tumors. However, as time passed, we had "forgotten" the threat when the cancer seemed to disappear. Then, in November, Jim discovered another lump and the doctors advised an amputation. We were all shocked and dazed. I resisted the surgery, holding out for another series of radiation treatments, but finally consented to Jim's wishes to be free of this terrible threat to his life. The monster would not let go of his grip on Jim's hand.

After endless consultations and midnight prayers, Jim decided to have the operation. My own unrelenting optimism led me to want him to try radiation—one more time. Yet, it was *his* arm and *his* decision. Had it been my own arm, I would have postponed amputation indefinitely, perhaps to my own detriment. With any kind of medical problem, I'm the Queen of Denial. I'd say to myself, "Oh, a lump...okay, I'll have it checked in three months." I'd just rather see whether I could beat the odds and live with it, rather than to chop off a part of my own body! It seemed so drastic to me. What I had to understood was that the blackness of the constant threat to his life was more threatening to Jim than not having an arm. It had to be his decision, but I still hoped that some doctor somewhere would recommend that Jim try radiation again. Anyhow, when my husband was ready to face the knife, I was determined to support him.

Before they rolled him into surgery, I removed his wedding ring from that hand, the one that would never again embrace me. It may sound strange, but I said goodbye and kissed the pale, troubled hand as I put the gold band on my own index finger. As I sat by his bedside waiting for him to awaken, I realized that if the cancer returned, I could be left alone for the rest of my life. I had always had the childlike belief that Dad would take care of me until I grew up and then

Mehr

Jim would always be there in his place. Now, I had to admit that neither of them was powerful enough to protect me or even themselves from disease and loss. I realized that I could be alone for the rest of my life, a single mother with four children.

Alone, in the recovery room, I sat in silence and wrote:

One Flesh

And the twain shall be one flesh.
One flesh?
The exultant coupling of youth:
Was that one flesh?

Then three, four, five, finally six —
Sweet babes so dear,
Fists grasped and hearts beating —
One flesh?

BROKEN CIRCUITS
A Memoir of Alzheimer's Disease in Four Voices

> Twenty plus years more
>
> In a white, white room
>
> With beeps and tubes,
>
> I curled beside him to make the passing
>
> > of the night more tolerable
> >
> > and shared his pain
>
> And knew one flesh.

Two of my friends went with me to the hospital to accompany me during the long hours of recovery. Jim didn't want me to leave his bedside, asking that I sit silently without talking. So, I did, but I was in anguish, totally locked inside myself with no way out. Then, when I did go home, someone might ask, "Hey, how are you doing?" and I would overflow with the sadness, grief, resentment I had just experienced in that square white room. The children, too, wanted me to be optimistic because they had only seen their Dad once during the week of his recovery. I told them, "Great, he's doing great. Everything is going to be fine," but I wasn't really convinced. I felt like I had to be everyone's cheerleader. It was all I could do

Mehr

to cope with my own problems. There wasn't time to worry about my parents.

Finally, Jim came home and the children and I all tried to be upbeat. One day, when I was trying to open up this large tin of rice, I became more and more frustrated, finally attacking the lid with a chisel and a screwdriver, then banging it on the counter. The damned thing still wouldn't budge and everytime I pounded I got even angrier that I didn't have enough strength to crack the seal. Finally, I just dropped the tin into the sink and rolled over onto the carpet and sobbed, realizing that for the rest of my life I would have to take care of everything that required two hands, everything! This tin barrel was just a small part of the whole crisis, but my failure to open it sparked all the feelings of helplessness I had felt since Jim first learned he had cancer. All I could think was, *there's no one to take care of me now. Dad is disappearing. Jim has lost his arm and I can't open this rice tin!* I covered my head with a pillow, as though I could protect myself from the fallout of this realization. A mushroom cloud hovered in the sky—for me, as ominous as Chernobyl—large, dark and menacing.

BROKEN CIRCUITS
A Memoir of Alzheimer's Disease in Four Voices

My husband didn't seem to care that he had just lost an arm and that I was on the floor under a pillow. He seemed like such a Happy-Jack, adjusting to the loss of his arm, teaching his classes, writing his books. I couldn't believe his sunny demeanor. Finally, when my oldest daughter, Susan, and I were moving one of the kid's mattresses into another room, stumbling around and banging into walls, he said, "Here, let me help you." And I said, "What can you do? You're helpless! You're just a one-armed man!" I was so frustrated that I lost control. It was a cruel thing to say to him and once I said it, I couldn't take it back. He had been wounded by the surgeon's knife and now, once more, by my words.

Maybe these eruptions are all about being human, but I still can't forgive myself. *Why did I have to be so cruel?* And why do I still have to cry when I write this? I guess because I haven't recovered from all that I lost—a belief in Jim's wholeness, my goodness, the security of our lives together. I wished that my father could support me, offer some kind words or a reassuring pat on the back, but he was struggling with his own battles. After a few months, Jim's recovery seemed complete. He had returned to the university, resumed writing his history books, riding his bicycle and even playing ball with the kids. I still haven't recovered my confidence. It was a real hard time.

Even though Dad had some impairments, I expected that my parents would rally to help whenever we asked. Since Jim and I needed to spend time away, to reconnect and heal from the injuries we had experienced, I called Mother. "Mom, I need to ask a favor. I need you to come and stay with the kids while Jim and I spend a week on the coast." It nearly knocked me off my chair when she didn't agree immediately. Mother said, "Why don't you see if you can find someone nearby and I'll help you pay her." I didn't want a nanny, I wanted my mother and whatever was left of my father.

I felt like telling her, "Look, Mom, I really need you and you won't come because it just isn't convenient." I rarely asked her to do anything, trying to be independent and self-sufficient and now that I really needed help, she was willing to write checks, but not to show up to give Jim and me a chance to get away. It wasn't Dad's fault because he would do whatever she decided, so as far as I was concerned, my mother was basically being selfish. All along, my father had been the generous one, not her, and without his urging, she was just plain selfish.

A few months after Mother turned down my request, Jim's wound had begun to heal and my anger was subsiding. I asked Mom again to visit us. I had hoped that she and Dad could stay with our two youngest children for a few days while we were gone and then for a week longer with us. At first, Mom said "I don't think so, Honey, we'll come when both of you are there." One more time, I felt hurt and angry, angry at myself for even asking her again. My friends could support me, in any way I asked, but my own mom wouldn't come to help me just five months later. And then, I began to think about how frightened she must be, watching Dad lose his mind, then seeing her son-in-law lose an arm. Maybe she just couldn't face another sorrowful situation alone.

Even if she was frightened, Mother called a few days later to say that she and Dad would be arriving the following week. I suspect that Marilyn probably interceded and gave her some backbone. Isn't it something that a daughter has to teach a mother how to be a mother? Yet, I realized that my own daughters have taught me a few things, so I tried to be less critical of Mom. She was facing some rough times.

My folks arrived, we dropped them off at our house and helped them to settle, then, Mother waited about two minutes after Jim and I said goodbye to "reorganize" our bedroom—sorted every letter, note, scrap of paper I had saved. When we came back to Huntsville days later, my anger came back like a firestorm. She had finally responded to my casting call for a mother by playing the role of the busybody! As a mother she was unable, as always, to respect my personal boundaries. When I saw what she had done, I blew up, telling her she had invaded my space, had no business in my bedroom and should mind her own business. She cringed as I said these things. "I was only trying to help out," she pleaded.

Finally, we declared a truce which allowed us to get along, tensely, but politely. Dad painted the garage door and Mom drove Heather to her piano lessons. I hoped we just might make it through the week without another eruption. Of course, I was wrong. Driving home from a day of teaching, I had no premonition of the scene that would greet me—three of the people I loved were drawn into a tug-of-war in front of our house—my son in the middle of my mother and father, each pulling on one of his arms—as they lurched back and forth across the driveway, shouting and yelling about how to get to Safeway's. "It's that way!" she screamed. "No, it's that way!" Dad roared, as he jerked my son free and fell against the crabapple tree.

I was livid. "Stop it, both of you! What the hell difference does it make, where the damned store is?" Neither answered, paralyzed by my anger. "I will NOT have the two of you acting like that in MY home. You've embarrassed me in front of the whole neighborhood and I won't stand for it, do you hear?"

Dad turned on his heel, headed for Safeway's or hell, I didn't care, and didn't return until dusk. He and Mother went upstairs and I could hear him yelling that he would not stay in my house one more night. "I will not tolerate this disrespect. She should get down on her knees and beg forgiveness for the way she spoke to me!" *Ha, fat chance,* I thought to myself. *Let them behave like the children they are. I've had it with their bickering.*

Mehr

Little did I realize that there was still another act in this melodrama. Later that night, Brad opened the gate and let our dog out, perhaps by accident, perhaps not. Dad heard him calling the dog and came lurching down the stairs, looking for a stick to beat my son. I blocked him at the bottom steps, hands on my hips and said, "*We* don't beat our kids and *you* won't beat them either." I was scared stiff, but I stared him down. He may have poisoned his own home, but he wasn't going to poison mine, Alzheimer's or not.

That weekend marked a time when I truly grew up. I was forty-two years old and had finally stood up to both of my parents, locking my mother out of my bedroom and declaring to my father, "You will not, you cannot act this way. This is *my* house and you two are not going to behave here the way you do at your house. I'm in charge of this house and I set the rules." They were both stunned because "Baby Judy" had grown up.

****

<u>Nancy:</u>

BROKEN CIRCUITS
A Memoir of Alzheimer's Disease in Four Voices

I looked out of my window at Mt. Timpanogas, listening to my mother's phone conversations about my father, trying to offer sympathy and support, but not feeling as though I had much to give her. I had a family of my own, one that needed some attention, too. My husband, Lee, had been complaining about chest pains ever since he was sent home a few months ago from his coaching job at a girls' camp. They had urged him to go home when he had complained to the staff about a pain in his upper left chest, but tough guy that he was, he waited until the afternoon to leave. When my oldest daughter, Lisa, who was nineteen and was working in a doctor's office, overheard his symptoms, she looked right at him and kept repeating, "Dad, you *need* to have that checked!"

Lee listened and nodded, but went right back to the camp where he began to put up a big tent for the kids. Suddenly, his pain began to radiate to his jaw. This time, he drove right home and I called the doctor. On Monday, August 10th, he flunked a treadmill test and was scheduled immediately for an appointment with a cardiologist in Provo the next day. Lee said, "Oh, I can't go tomorrow because I have some things I need to do in Salt Lake." The doctor said, "Well, this is important. You're a forty-seven year old man with chest pain. You're going to see a cardiologist tomorrow!"

The cardiologist put him in the hospital at once. His angiogram showed a 96% blockage, so he was scheduled for an angioplasty the next day. My son, Pete, and I watched the monitor as they performed the procedure. It seemed strange, but I could see fluid spraying throughout the whole chest cavity. Lee kept saying, "My back hurts," to which the nurses would respond, "I'm sorry, my friend, but we'll take care of your back pain when we get you upstairs."

I know I was tense about everything, but I worried as the medical team took longer and longer to give him more blood thinner. I started to wonder, *why are they taking so long to do this procedure?* Finally, one of the doctors told him, "There's a flap in one of your arteries and we were hoping that we could seal it off, but everytime your heart pumps, the flap opens." So, they gave him some morphine, sent me home and scheduled surgery for the next day. Of course, he was in pain all night because there was a build-up of pressure when his heart beat. Just before his open heart surgery, he called me at 5:00 a.m., asking me to come to the hospital. I drove through

BROKEN CIRCUITS
A Memoir of Alzheimer's Disease in Four Voices

the early dawn, thinking dark thoughts such as, *What if he dies? What will I do?* I I needed help to be strong and I needed it now. In the early stillness of the morning, I parked the van and knelt down and prayed. As I did so, I felt an inner strength and peace. Once inside the hospital, I walked alongside his gurney as far as the operating room knowing that I could handle whatever might happen.

In a few hours, the doctor came out smiling, saying everything had gone well. The surgeons had repaired the tear in the artery and tightened the flap. I was relieved and tired, but I went to Intensive Care to sit with Lee when he awoke from anesthesia. He awakened and was still foggy, muttering that he was sorry, but he had died. I laughed and squeezed his hand, telling him he was very much alive, then he nodded off and I went to find a nurse. As I was talking to her, I heard a beep-beep-beep. Suddenly, people in white descended from every corner of the floor, running to Lee's room as the nurse led me to a chair, explaining that my husband had just pulled all his tubes out. Lee hadn't remembered the anesthetic, had felt tied down by the i.v. tubes and then yanked all of them from his chest and arms in one swift jerk. The place went berserk!

Nurses and doctors arrived at once. I watched them working furiously to reattach the tubes and sustain his blood pressure. Suddenly, I realized that my husband was dying. *He's dying right before me!* One of the nurses called down to the Operating Room from the CCU, and I could hear her saying, "What a shame...he was so young, only forty-seven years old." I realize that they had given up. They didn't think they could save him. Only one of them kept trying, a young Filipino doctor who began jamming more tubes back into Lee's arms until somehow, my dear, sweet "suicidal" husband responded.

After we went home, Lee was unable to teach for two and a half months, giving us precious time alone together. We would walk a little farther every day, getting to know some of the neighbors we had never met. He became a little stronger every day, reassuring our kids who had been hysterical throughout most of this crisis. When Lee was in the hospital, my two middle daughters, Carrie and Sarah, ages twelve and fourteen, took a whitewater river rafting trip together, causing some of their friends to respond, "I can't believe you're doing this. Your Dad's in the hospital and you're going camping!" I understood why they needed to leave—their father could die—and urged them to go. My oldest son Pete disappeared, too for awhile, and my second son Nate didn't come around either. None of them wanted to face the possibility of losing their father. My oldest daughter Lisa was the only one who was mature enough to visit Lee often with her friends, who told him funny stories, and brought silly gifts.

My parents didn't offer to support me and I didn't ask them to, especially after our blow-up after their anniversary party. My four girls, who were all living at home, were helpful in doing household tasks and many of my neighbors brought food. I was coping well enough, and on the day that Lee was scheduled to have the angiogram, I even went to a barbecue at the church. When I told the Bishop that the procedure was scheduled for the next day, he seemed to be shocked that I was there, aware that Lee's condition was serious enough that we could lose him. I must have been in shock myself, because I didn't think it was a big deal. The doctors had reassured me that my husband's chances were 95% positive, so I didn't worry.

Finally, in December of 1988, Mom and Dad came to see us. I hadn't wanted them to visit while Lee was recovering from his surgery because they would have just been two more people to look after. Yet, when my second son, Nate, decided to go on a two-year mission for the church, I thought the time was right. I invited them to join us for his farewell even though my folks usually avoided winter visits because they hated snow and ice. This time they wanted to make the sacrifice because they were so proud of their grandson.

A few days after they arrived, Dad disappeared from our house. We all assumed he had gone for a walk; however, no one had seen him leave—and the temperatures were probably in the low 40's. We all started looking around the nearby streets, and somebody phoned Kountry Korner, our local gas station and convenience store. When asked if an older man with white hair and a plaid flannel shirt were there, they said, "Sure, he's here, over in the corner having a cup of coffee and a donut." In a few minutes, Nate and a couple of his friends arrived, looking for their Grandpa. They could see that

BROKEN CIRCUITS
A Memoir of Alzheimer's Disease in Four Voices

Dad was cold and confused, so they brought him right home to warm up. Maybe my second son was growing up, I thought as I watched him gently help my father out of the car and guide him up the driveway.

On the Sunday of the "farewell" church service in Nate's honor, we asked Dad to give a prayer to open the meeting, a simple task for him as long as he could find a few well-worn grooves in his brain. Lee and I sat beside him on the podium ready to cue him if necessary. After the opening hymn, we gestured to Dad to stand up and offer the prayer. He was nervous and apparently confused, but he walked up to the podium and started to talk. He told everyone how thankful he was to be there on this occasion, which was fine, but it wasn't a prayer. I stood up beside him whispering that he was supposed to pray, not give a speech. He closed his eyes and I slowly coached him through the prayer, feeding him sentences as though he were a small child. It was during this experience that I first noticed that he used the phrase "on this occasion" to hide the fact that he did not *know* what the *occasion* was. He repeated this phrase often in the years that followed. As I stood at his side that day, I felt a return of the tenderness I had experienced at the lake a few years before. Many people commented to me later that I had treated my father with such gentleness and love. Perhaps, one day, I might even forgive him for the whole Christmas debacle.

For the first time in my life, I realized that I could lose both my father and my husband. Of course, I had known that they would die, as we all do, but I hadn't ever allowed myself to feel how bereft I would be. I wanted to hold on to them fiercely, to heal them and make them whole. If only I could protect them from weakness, infirmity and yes, even death.

****

<u>Dennis:</u>
After the anniversary, when we were still trying to keep up the pretense that Dad could still work, Mom would drive him back and forth to the office, or the "White House," as we called the little frame cottage behind the store. She would write the checks for the payables and he would answer phones and file invoices. My job was to show up every few hours to referee their fighting. In this way, we struggled through the *transition* from work to *pretend-work*.

BROKEN CIRCUITS
A Memoir of Alzheimer's Disease in Four Voices

I have letters that he wrote to suppliers that show how hard he and his brain were trying to hook up. Sometimes, I tried to imagine how I would feel if my brain were becoming unwired—like a coma, like a Hitchcock movie, like a Spielberg movie, like a bad dream!!! If only there were a fuse I could replace to make his brain work.

One day, while Dad tried to open the door to the White House, with the keys I had colored to match the locks, Mother got frustrated and grabbed the keys from him. He was unprepared for this sudden action and responded like an animal. He lunged at her, striking her shoulder, knocking her off the porch and onto the grass. Next, Mom comes to her son in his shop where he is waiting on customers at the counter, crying, "Your father just knocked me down." *Damn—what to do?*

Hug Mom, ignore customers. Hug Mom, put Mom out of sight, look for Dad, find Dad, unlock door, look out, seat Dad who, by the way, doesn't remember hitting Mom. Put large stock of paper in front of Dad, look for Mom, find Mom, tell Mom it will be okay, get Mom and Dad in same room, try to sell a few auto parts. Everybody's okay...one more day.

Mehr

"All in a day's work," you might say, but there was always one more "night's work" when I got home. While my mother and father were fighting one last battle for control, my own family was falling apart. My wife and I were drinking way too much, but she was in a lot more trouble than I was. I had seen the problem coming for a long time, like a slow-moving tsunami headed toward the shore, but I kept hoping it would never arrive. Our marriage was in serious trouble.

We were both nineteen when we got married, Linda and I, too young for sure, but I was in the Air Force and we were both so lonesome without each other. I was not only too young, I was stupid…probably just lonesome…just reached out, too soon before I had even started to grow up. At first, the two of us were fine, made friends at the base at Lackland, had our first child, Bryan, and then we came back to L.A.

I know I'm not a storybook husband and I wasn't always there when I should have been. If there were ever an opportunity to have fun, I never passed it by. There wasn't a right and wrong, I just got involved with whoever or whatever was happening. Linda should have said something to me, thrown me out, divorced me, but she needed me too much. I'm her security and she wouldn't do it. She would have another drink.

After we moved into the house in Fullerton, I lost a lot of money and both of us started drinking seriously. I didn't see what was happening when Linda started to act strange, refusing to get out of bed in the mornings, having these crying jags. At first, I thought she had a thyroid problem, then an estrogen imbalance after her hysterectomy. Finally, I realized that the problem was depression and alcohol and told her, but she wouldn't get help.

Jennifer left home when she was eighteen because she didn't want anymore of the mess we had created, and I guess that's why Bryan left, too. When Linda went out at night, I never knew whether she would come back. Once, she crashed the car in Craig Park and I found her sitting in a stream in her bra and underwear. When I put her in Brea Hospital, it was supposed to be because she was depressed, but it was really because she was drunk, yet the doctors didn't catch on for a very long time. There was a war going on inside her and her only remedy was alcohol.

Mehr

For awhile we were two of the beautiful people of Orange County. I've been told that I'm good looking, tall, athletic, with a strong Irish face like my uncles on my mother's side, and my wife was one of those blonde, Southern California cheerleader-types, talkative, exhuberant and fun. We joined Sunny Hills Racquet Club, and drank with the best of them, all the young, up-and- coming country club crowd. Finally, it all got to be too much. First, her parents both died, then her depression got worse, so she drank more and got more depressed. I didn't know what to do, so I drank, too. It's a sad story. Obviously, I couldn't pay a lot of attention to my folks unless they punched each other out in front of our store. Then, I had to do something. The rest of the time I was running a 911 rescue operation for my tormented little bride.

****

Marilyn:

Betty and I were delirious when our agent called to say that our book proposal had sold. The two of us had been working for over a year to shape our research into a proposal about women graduates of Hunter College High School over the past century.

BROKEN CIRCUITS
A Memoir of Alzheimer's Disease in Four Voices

We had stumbled upon the idea on a winter trip to Mammoth ski resort where we had planned to meet some friends for Christmas and cross-country skiing. After six hours of driving we were almost to the lodge when a trooper made us turn back, explaining that an avalanche had blocked the road. Fortunately, we found a room in a Best Western where we unpacked, ate a Christmas eve dinner of fried chicken and baked potatoes, and warmed ourselves before the large fireplace in the lobby of the hotel.

One of the unexpected benefits of an accident is that it sometimes forces us to sit still. Beneath the scheduling and busyness of so much activity is a vast accretion of memory and insight which we hardly ever tap, unless forced to. As Betty and I sat by the fire, we began to release the demands of our complex lives and recall important people and events from our past, sharing stories we had never taken the time to tell each other. When Betty recalled how she had traveled from the Bronx to Manhattan every day to attend Hunter College High School, I found the story intriguing. How had she found the courage to leave her neighborhood, face the competition from other bright girls whose parents had far more education, wealth and status? And what had happened to all the other smart girls who had taken four years of Latin, science, math and history? We didn't have the answers but were fascinated by the questions.

We never made it to the ski resort, but as soon as we returned from our trip we approached the questions in true academic form. We received start-up funds from USC School of Education, then published a preliminary report which was reviewed by Grace Hechinger at *Glamour Magazine.* Our phones rang for days. One of the most important calls was from Barbara Lowenstein, who became our agent and sold the book to Simon and Schuster. Little did we realize the unexpected benefits of an avalanche.

Betty's life had been completely altered by taking advantage of the opportunity to attend a first-rate school. Had her sixth grade teacher failed to recognize her student's gifts, had her mother been unable to imagine a brighter future for her daughter, had Betty herself lacked the bravery to cross a cultural divide wider than the East River, she probably would have lived a very tiny life in a flat little box in the Bronx. She was not alone in experiencing the transformation that an education can offer. We interviewed other women like herself—bright, well-educated and insightful. They ranged in age from nineteen to ninety. What they all shared was a common launching pad composed of dedicated teachers who drew upon the rich resources of New York City. We were touched by their stories, curious about their successes and failures, warmed by their willingness to be so vulnerable. When Simon and Schuster bought the book we were ready to write.

First, we took our own Sabbaticals. Betty had earned a year off from USC to complete her research, and I decided to buy my own freedom by resigning my position at the family practice residency program where I had been a psychologist for almost a decade. As a psychologist, I was proud of my work, nine years at Children's Hospital, then nine more at Glendale. I had met with countless patients whose lives were affected by illness and suffering, met with students and residents to teach them what I knew about compassion and healing, met with many faculty members to negotiate our interests in teaching and research. There had been moments of tremendous satisfaction, but also many of frustration and sadness, primarily with the politics of professional life.

I was ready to try something new. Both Betty and I had been drawn to Washington State on several holiday visits, so we looked northward to find a writing home for our year ahead. Bainbridge Island seemed perfect—small, forested, rural—but close enough to Seattle to provide culture and friendship. In one short weekend, we sold our old and beloved mountain home in Idyllwild and put our our suitcases and Siberian Husky, Tasha, in the car and headed for a year's adventures on an island in Puget Sound.

In the midst of so much good fortune, I still felt a sense of unease, perhaps of dread, a reverberating signal that the future might not be trusted. Perhaps, my Grandmother Lena had felt this same sense of foreboding when she left her little Swiss village of St. Gallen, at the turn of the century. In all of my grandmother's exhilaration, was there a current of dread humming in the background like a minor chord? Had she listened or did she dismiss the monody of warning? I was aware of my fears, but attributed them to something concrete— our move.

BROKEN CIRCUITS
A Memoir of Alzheimer's Disease in Four Voices

Betty hadn't noticed my anxiety. She had just been invited to give a keynote speech for the National Association of the Teachers of Gifted Children and was preparing for the trip. Following the article in *Glamour,* she had been interviewed on radio and TV stations around the country and h invited to speak at several conferences on educating gifted children. We both enjoyed the attention she was receiving. After years of teaching at U.S.C as a professor, she finally had the opportunity to speak to a larger audience. It was a stressful time, but an exciting one and we both anticipated the year ahead.

The Idyllwild house had sold much too quickly for me. It was here in the shadow of the San Jacinto mountains that I had overcome the heavy baggage of fear and anxiety over writing, and enrolled in a workshop on the Isomata campus led by a wise and trusted friend, Norman Corwin. A truly gifted journalist with years of experience as a war correspondent, radio announcer, scriptwriter and playwright, Norman was patient as a teacher. He sat quietly listening as his students read, resting against a gray river rock fireplace in his flannel shirt and corduroys, his white hair framing a lined face with cobalt blue eyes. It was his enthusiasm that rekindled the confidence my mother had offered to me as a child whenever I would ready my writing. "My daughter's going to be a writer," she would tell her friends. "Let me read you one of her poems!"

In a few years, well-meaning college teachers stamped out some of that confidence, as they edited, rearranged, criticized my work, insisting on a sterile flatness in style and tone. I had been traumatized by these teachers and it took someone like Norman to awaken me from my slumber. He was my sweet prince.

I've always had a sixth sense that has led me to what psychologists like to call "transition objects." Religious people call them priests or gurus, while mountaineers call them guides or Sherpas. Whatever the term, I have found in uncles, teachers, therapists and sometimes friends, the profound belief in my worth and ability that pushes me toward another challenge. Norman was there when I needed him. His response was critical. Had he wavered for a moment in his enthusiasm for my work, I would have returned to my life as a psychologist and teacher content to expand my curiosity through travelling and professional research.

BROKEN CIRCUITS
A Memoir of Alzheimer's Disease in Four Voices

Following our writing workshop with Norman, Betty and I wrote a proposal about women like ourselves, our mothers, our aunts and sisters who had never realized their potential. We were packing in a frenzy, loading boxes, taping packages, dodging an anxious dog, Tasha the Siberian, who watched for signs that she might be left behind. Betty had been sitting at her desk in the corner of the dining room typing her speech for the National Gifted Children's conference when she suddenly stopped and began rubbing her forehead. I sensed that something was wrong and asked if everything was all right.

"No, it's not," she said softly, "I can't see."

"What do you mean, *you can't see?* Are you saying you can't see light or shadows, or what? Anything or nothing?" I was trying to wall off a rush of panic that seemed to be lifting me from the floor. The earth was shifting as if signalling a massive earthquake. Fine, I just wanted to be standing in a doorway.

"I can't see a thing."

I watched her as she rolled her eyes in four directions, pressed her eyelids as she tried again to see and couldn't.

Mehr

"You must have had a stroke. Let's get the hell out of here. I'm taking you to the hospital."

"No, you're not. I'm going to lie down for awhile and you're going to pack these boxes into the car. We'll put the dog in last and then we'll leave." She waved me on, then stood up, touching the backs of the chairs as markers as she shuffled to the couch where she lay down.

"I'm sorry I can't help, but you'd better get busy. The new owners will take possession tomorrow, remember?"

I protested and threatened, but she wouldn't be moved. She lay there, eyes closed, inert and incommunicado. Yes, I told myself as I watched her breathe, I could *force* her to go, drag her kicking and fighting through the house and press her into the car. Or, I could do what she asks, finish the packing, load the dog and her into the car and drive to a doctor's office. But who? *Sam, dear friend in times of crisis, I will call Sam.* My hands were shaking as I dialed his number and waited as it rang, two, three, four times, before he answered.

"Sam, I want Betty to see a doctor in two hours. She's blind, can't see…no, not a thing. We're coming down the hill from Idyllwild and I want an appointment today."

He asked questions about her health, trauma, medications, then told me he would find someone. I knew he would.

Before I started the motor on the Jimmy, Sam called, spoke to Betty and told her that I was driving her to see a neurologist. He spoke slowly and enunciated every word. "Betty, listen to me. I am a physician and I am telling you to get in the car, drive down the mountain and go directly to Dr. Cynthia Lee's office. I will now call her and she will be expecting you. Got it?"

"Got it," she said, and let me lead her to the car.

For two hours, I tried to fill the time by telling her about the scenery, the traffic, the colors of the sky. If I kept talking, I told myself, I could stampede the fear that was crawling up my spine. *What if this is a stroke? What if she never sees again? Can Tasha be trained to guide her? What else can I do? I can't feel this helpless!*

In two hours, we were parking on Chevy Chase Boulevard next to a three-story office building. In two minutes we were in the waiting room, and in twenty minutes, Betty emerged on the arm of the nurse, eyes bandaged, laughing at the grim situation she now faced.

"It's an existential thing," she joked, once we were back in the car. "It might get better, or it might get worse. That is an informed expert opinion. One thing we know is that it's not a stroke, so it could be worse. I could have had an aneurysm. Bad news, the optic nerves are inflamed and they might not recover."

Oh, I see. Unpack the car, deliver Betty, fix dinner and answer the phone. My brother tells me that Dad has run a red light on Garfield, narrowly escaping a sixteen-wheeler before crashing into a brick wall. Oh.

***

CHAPTER SEVEN

LOSS AND RECOVERY (1989-90)

> <u>Sept. 2, 1989,</u> Tues, pt. fell, shopping with wife, in Downey, says "World is basically on a downhill." He feels that taking medicine is like taking dope. Pt. denies memory problems. Only problem is not enough money.
>
> <u>9/14/89</u> Worsening cognitive state, tone seems more confused. Wife under stress, starting to admit losses. Mini-mental status 16/30
>
> <u>2/3/90</u> Neurology consult: Gradual deterioration in memory, but still functions well in the home setting, walks the dog, goes to the store, but can't remember a list of short items. Knows the President but not the year. Does not remember that this is a hospital. H. Choi, M.D.

Mehr

<u>Marilyn:</u>

When Dr. Brummel-Smith had advised Dad against driving two years earlier, Dad continued anyway. He had passed his driver's exam given by The Rancho without a mistake. My brother had found a motor vehicles agent who gave Dad an oral exam which he had also somehow passed. Dennis felt guilty enough about Dad's accident that he was willing to let me lift the car keys for good.

My brother filled in the details of the accident a few days after the event. By the time I had arrived, my parents had been sent home and I had put them to bed and saved my questions for later. I called my brother.

"What happened, Den?"

"He ran straight through a red light on Gardendale and Garfield and right through a brick fence. Mother called me and I got to the emergency room right away."

"How was he?"

"Awful...flat on his back on a gurney, his head laced with black stitches...eyes all hollowed out and dark...He just looked so weak."

"Did he recognize you?"

He paused, stifling a sob. "Yeah, he took my hand and I thought, *I got him the damned license."*

"Yes, you did," I said gently. "Now, it's time to take it away."

Who wants to take away the keys from a parent? Who wants to be the one to say, "That's the end of you and your red Ford pickup?" Not me. But, after several phone calls with my sisters and brother, I realized that I was the one who must take action. They would support me, but they didn't want to look Dad in the eye and tell him his driving days were over.

I had intended to talk to him two years ago, but he had driven to Utah and seemed to make few mistakes. Then, there were a couple of near-misses, lapses in concentration, until now he had glided through a red light, barely dodging a large truck and run into a brick wall. The next one could be fatal, not only to Dad, but to others. It was time to take they keys. I asked him and Mother to lunch, brought up the accidents and insisted that the time had come for him to learn how to be a good passenger. Mother hid her face in her napkin, trying not to show her tears, but surprisingly, he accepted my conclusion. He sighed, looked out the window at the traffic on the Long Beach Freeway and handed me his keys. After all, he was the one that had hit the wall. It was his head that the doctors had bandaged.

He was also losing his kind and stalwart family physician, Dr. Brummel-Smith. Ken had accepted another job offer from Oregon and would no longer be Dad's doctor. A nice woman, Dr. Choi, had tried to take Ken's place. She was attentive and solicitous, but her focus was on the medical details, rather than the social and familial ones where we needed the most help. Ken had filled a special place in our lives, coaching, advising, offering hope and resources. Now, he was gone and we had to continue his work ourselves.

****

<u>Judy:</u>

Marilyn called me to say that Dad had recovered from his accident, given up his car keys forever and seemed content to stay close to home. My husband Jim was continuing to recover from his cancer operation and I felt I could pay attention to my father. As Dad continued to slip away, I tried desperately to salvage whatever glimpses of recognition or memory I could. In fact, as part of an assignment in a journal writing class, I wrote a letter to a father who would never read it. I didn't send it because I feared it might hurt him. Then what would he do? Cry, probably, and then what? Sit there staring at the words in silence. I couldn't bear to think of him that way. So, I wrote the letter for myself, read it aloud in class. I cried, they all cried and, for awhile, I felt some relief.

Dear Dad,   Summer, 1989

I think of you often and wonder if it makes you as sad as it makes us to see all you've lost in the last six years. You worked so hard all your life to build a business, a home, a position of some status and respect, and the years are robbing all those good feelings from you.

At first, we'd all laugh and say, "It's hell getting old and forgetting things." Even when Mom finally knew that it was more serious than that, we didn't listen because it seemed to be just her hypercritical way of carping at you.

When you hit that big truck, we knew you couldn't continue to drive. It's so hard for me to think of stripping away your dignity and taking the keys to the red Ford pick-up. We understand that you're a different man now—physically

Mehr

healthy and pretty robust for 78—but there's so little left of you.

Our girls, Susan and Karin, knew you when you were still outlandish and plain-spoken. They had never known anyone who would curse in mid-sentence and use words that are absolutely taboo in their social circles. I had. It was YOU, and I wasn't amused. I have to struggle so to remember nice things, warm things, but here are a few:

—You always forgot the exact date of my birthday, so you would bring me home a card or a trinket for three or four days. I sat on the corner waiting for you to drive up in the red truck, stop and let me and my friends jump onto the sideboards and ride the rest of the way home. I could hear the sounds of the milk bottles rattling in their metal cages as we bumped together along the asphalt road.

—I remember how you would tell us each Christmas about living on Captain Abbott's farm when you were a boy. Your family was so poor that there were no gifts except the candy and apples that the Captain brought. You always cried when you told the story, tears that welled up from an old mix of anguish and gratitude.

BROKEN CIRCUITS
A Memoir of Alzheimer's Disease in Four Voices

—You were always generous with money. You worked hard for it, but you gave it to us freely when we asked. We never felt the sting of poverty.

My son Bradley will never really know you, but I think you would like him if you had the time. You like his dad a lot and he'll be like him. He's a sweet, sensitive boy, always ready with a hug and a wet kiss. He likes games and stories, especially, the ones about Grandpa's childhood. He knows you get confused and irritated with him when he wins at checkers or teases too much or too long, but he has good memories, too.

I wish you could tell us about when you were young again, Dad, tell the stories one more time—about the pony, the funny schoolteacher who tried to teach you to march, the accident with the hay rake which tore off your little toe, the Indians and the hard crusts of bread. Can you remember, Dad? Please...tell us the stories one more time, Dad, so you'll remember and we'll remember.

Love, Judy

I know I should have told Dad these things while he was able to understand and remember them. My excuse was that I was busy, busy raising kids, busy getting a degree, busy in my church, but the truth was, I was still afraid of him, afraid to get too close, afraid of the memories of childhood when he tickled and kissed me, how he couldn't keep his hands off from me. I didn't tell him and I finally just ran away from him.

My children didn't know about those times. They just knew they were losing a grandfather, a funny old man who had been both generous and mean, but who had been part of their lives. They were trying to capture their grandfather, collecting photographs, boxing up his letters and taping conversations. My daughter Karin, who was the family historian, went to Los Angeles during Spring break and interviewed Dad to record his few remaining memories. While he faded in and out at times, he was mostly lucid. She asked him about his life, his family and his travels. He appeared to be taking stock of his life, weighing the good and the not-so-good.

Although Mother and Dad were able to travel to several countries after his retirement, he particularly remembered the trip that he and a fellow church member, Fred Williams, took to South America in 1965. In Buenos Aires, he met Graciela Bazet-White, the foreign exchange student who lived with our family for one year when she and I were both seniors. "Gracie," as we called her, touched all of our lives, and his recollections of her are still vivid and poignant.

In the interview, Karin returned to her own relationship with Dad, reflecting on how similar their personalities are, especially when they lose their tempers. When she told him that she is sometimes temperamental because she has his blood in her, he laughed heartily. Then she remarked that she is happy to have his blood in her and he chuckled to hold back tears. In the following transcript, I also record my own thoughts as I listened to the tape.

He began speaking about his last year in high school. "I went to school through the tenth grade in a one-room schoolhouse. We lived out in the country and hadn't learned how to behave." There is a pause as he chuckles to himself. "We played a lot of tricks on the teachers."

Uh-huh, and each of your three daughters has become a teacher. Didn't we show you!

He continued. "Well, the teacher wasn't any good, so we ran him out of town, just chased him out of town on our ponies…" He reflected for a few minutes, and then admitted,

Mehr

"It was a bad thing to do because he was sick, but we were kids and didn't care. He shouldn't have been teaching anyway, because he was an ignorant man."

An ignorant man, I see, so you run him out of town, do you? A bunch of stupid kids run an "ignorant" man, the only teacher in their godforsaken wilderness, out of town! In spite of myself, I laugh. This is so like him and his anti-authoritarian manner. I can just see him standing up in church, his thick frame planted in the aisles, telling the brethren how wrong they are, like the time they wanted to excommunicate my friend, Martha, who was six months pregnant and unmarried. And I'm just like him. I'm proud to admit it, but still ashamed. It's the injustice that always bothers me and I guess that's what got to him, too.

"My dad and mother were from a foreign country and they made a bare living. My Mother washed clothes for other people. She had immigrated from Switzerland and she just didn't know what to do, so she got by working for others who often took advantage of her. She was a very kind and real person, but Dad was kind of a misfit. He had come from

Switzerland, too, and had tried to farm, but he didn't know anything about farming, and he never fit in."

I see...You had this immigrant father who had been trained as a textile worker who is converted to the Mormon church, sent to the wilds of Eastern Utah to farm and doesn't fit in. Of course not, how could he? And how could he have taught you anything about fitting in? You tell people off, explode when angry, tease your children...did all of that happen to you?

"My father was much less of a provider than mother. He just took the attitude that that's the way it is and you can't do a thing about it. And both of them had language trouble, you know? Neither of them could speak English. They just believed in the gospel and thought that all they had to do was come to Salt Lake and they would be taken care of some way. That's not the way it goes..."

No, it usually isn't, but you still have to deal with the disappointment and rage that follows. Two hard-working but poor immigrants come to the U.S, thinking their lives will improve and end up washing clothes and mowing hay in the Uintah Basin. Interesting, isn't it, that I teach immigrants how to speak English? I thought I chose this field and now I think maybe it has chosen me.

"I'll tell you about the church. It has many loopholes. For one thing, it's a class system, you could say. If you're somebody, why you're *somebody.* If you're not, why you're *not.* If you go to church and you don't know how to talk or what to say, like my parents, it's pretty bad, even now."

Yes…I love my church, too, but there is always this issue of class…

"When I was fifteen years old, I left home. I decided that there wasn't anything worthwhile in that miserable dustbowl. And there was no way to make a living for yourself. I wanted out of there to see if I could do a little better so I went out over the hill. I didn't know and went to the mines in Bingham, halfway to Provo."

Fifteen years old—same age as my son Brad. Could I let him "go over the hill" tomorrow morning with no job, just a possibility for work in the mines? Not for a minute! No wonder you had such little sympathy for "whiners." You do what you have to do…

BROKEN CIRCUITS
A Memoir of Alzheimer's Disease in Four Voices

"There were a lot of men in line looking for jobs at the mine. Every once in a while, one of the foremen would appear and the guy who yelled, "mucker," got the job. So, of course the next time the foreman appeared, I yelled, "mucker," even though I had no idea what it meant, but I got the job. Then, I found out. The mucker's the one who throws the coal on the train way down deep in the ground—all day long—breaks your back. I took it for three months, then I decided that there wasn't anything to that, either, so I went to work for my brother, Otto, in Logan. That's where I kind of fell in love with a blonde gal whose name was Vivian. When I had a chance to go to Dayton, in Ohio, I talked her into getting married and off we went, without a nickel or a penny."

These two people who have lived in the same house for nearly fifty years, who have arisen at the same hour, kept the same schedule, gone to the same church on Sunday mornings, once took a risk. On a cold January day in 1936, they put a few belongings into a Model-A Ford and drove away, leaving friends and family, for an unknown place, "somewhere in Ohio." When I think of them lodged in front of the t.v. every night watching the news at exactly 6:30, I can hardly imagine their driving away from Logan, but they did. They were young once, and maybe even in love!

"Once we got to Dayton, we met some people who were in the church and before long, I was the Branch President. It was new and exciting. I hadn't had any experience in leading other people, but I believed I could do it. We were doing pretty well in the church and on the job, too, But, you have to remember that when you get to the point where you think things are going well and get a little proud, why, that's when trouble begins..."

Well, Dad at least you've gone back to the church...maybe your religion will help you to face what's coming.

"We had done well in the knitting mills in Dayton, so my brother sent me to go to California and set up another branch. We just packed up everything and went. Then the War came along and the business went bust. Nobody wanted wool dresses and we couldn't get any contracts for uniforms, so the whole thing went bust. I got by, though, one step ahead of the draft, running a milk truck, selling insurance, welding joints in the hold of aircraft carriers. Then, after the war, I bought my own business in Bell Gardens, auto parts, and that's where I stayed for forty years…"

Why does this bring tears? A governess and a textile worker marry, homestead in eastern Utah, have three sons, one of whom becomes a manager in a "textile" factory which fails, then he flails about, finds an opportunity and makes something of it for "forty years." This story is told in a matter-of-fact way that implies, "Well, that's what people do. They don't have time to wonder what color their parachute is, they just find work, they make a business, and they go to work at 7:00 a.m. every day for forty years.

Anyhow, time marches on and you get older and you feel like, I'm not sorry, but I've made a lot of mistakes in my life. Some of them were learning mistakes, and each time I made a mistake I tried to do better. I've had my own business and I've made it work."

Yes, you have…

"My wife? Vivian's a great gal…and she's put up with a lot from me. When I'm thinking right, I give her a lot of credit for all that's happened. We both have a temper, but we always get squared away when the time comes...yep. Now, I don't know where else I could go if I didn't have her."

I needed to hear you say this, Dad, that you loved mother and needed her. There were so many times when you two argued and bickered, that I had doubted whether you cared for each other at all.

"Vivian and I traveled a lot when I retired. We went to Ireland to visit her roots, then to Switzerland. It made me proud to see the country, the mountains and the people. I had never imagined the beauty of it. The trip that affected me most was the one I took to Peru, with Fred Williams. In Lima, we met a group of street urchins who surrounded our taxi. Their clothing was torn and they were obviously malnourished. Fred interpreted so I could talk to the taxi driver, Pedro Mendez, who arranged to buy food and clothing for the boys when I sent him money. I believe he took care of the boys, because he sent me pictures of the kids for many years. Everytime I received a packet of these photos I would cry. I was just so grateful that I could relieve their misery."

How can I stay angry at you when I hear this? Big crybaby, heart as big as Peru, trying in your own simple way to take care of a few boys, just as you tried to take care of us. Right now, I think I love you.

"After that, I went to Argentina. I wanted to go there because that little girl was there…Gracie. Seeing Gracie and her family was the culmination of the whole trip. She was just like my little girl and her family made me feel that I was the king everywhere I went. They just loved me and did everything they could for me."

He sighed and fell silent for awhile. "How do you get by in life? You just try to get along with people. That's A-1." Then, he asked Karin, "Are you a temperamental gal?"

"Yes, but not as bad as my mother. I've got your blood in me, what do you expect?"

"Well, I hope it's worth something."

"It's worth a lot, Grandpa. You're a wonderful man."

"Bless your heart, you don't know how much that means to me."

Or you to me, Dad.

****

<u>Nancy:</u>

Mehr

For a couple of years after the anniversary party, I could see how my parents continued to struggle with the demands of Dad's worsening condition. I tried to visit as often as I could, flying from Utah to Los Angeles every four or five months for a brief stay. Mom looked tired. She insisted on doing most of the caretaking, but the effects of her constant attention to Dad's needs were showing. Dad would go in and out of a coherent state almost instantaneously. One minute, he would tell me, "Nancy, you're a nice guy," and in the next, he would call me "Bootie," my nickname from toddlerhood. Mom bullied and ridiculed him, but I just sloughed it off. I realized that he had no future. He had begun to hide from her by pretending to be asleep most of the time. As he said to me one day, "What kind of a life is this?"

Once, when Mom and Dad and I were alone at the house, he and mother became argumentative about whether it was time to "go home" or not. Dad wanted to "go home," and Mother would say, "We *are* home!" Then he would say, "No, we're not," and so on, endlessly. I decided to take him with me to to a fast-food place, called Pollo Loco, to distract him from his obsession and get him out of Mother's way. He was willing to go with me, but he wanted Mother to come along, too, just to know where she was. Anyhow, his one last thrust was to remind Mother that she *was* his wife.

He said, "Vivian, you *are* my wife!"

And she responded, "That may be, but I'm still not going!"

He got mad, we took a drive to buy dinner, he forgot his anger and finally, recognized his home again.

I had to be the "peacemaker" now, although I was beginning to feel like the Pollo Loca myself. Mom assumed more control as Dad lost more of his. She controlled his diet rigidly and got mad if he ate too much fruit because his bowels were so loose that he would have "accidents," which she would angrily clean up. One time we were all three dozing in front of the television when Dad got up and sneaked to the kitchen. He practically inhaled a banana, in fear that Mom would wake up and yell at him for eating again. I watched him and grinned while Mom snored on. Little triumphs.

It was about this time that I realized that Mom was competing for popularity. Perhaps she always had been. She used to say that Dad put other people down to make himself feel better about himself. But she then put him down. *Which one was sicker?* I, who had always taken my mother's side, began to see how each enjoyed the constant scrimmaging.

Another time, I followed Dad on a circuitous route to the bathroom while Mom slept. He rolled out of his recliner with his usual apprehension over coordinating his movements and at first, turned toward the kitchen; then, before he could find the bathroom, feces started dropping from his pants leg onto the floor. I wiped him off, cleaned the linoleum and hoped Mom wouldn't see what had happened. As I rinsed out a towel, I turned to watch her still sleeping in the chair. One less attack in a lifetime of marital battles. I had maintained a fragile peace.

****

Marilyn:

I awakened to a winter storm. Sleet-colored waves lashed against the bulwark in front of the old Victorian house where Betty and I now lived. From the bedroom window, I could see the sky merge with the sea, a murky brew of mist and fog. For the first time since we had moved to Bainbridge Island for our year's sabbatical, I hadn't slept well. Today was my birthday, October 8, 1990, and I had spent a fitful night of dreaming, torturous dreams filled with haunting visitations from dead friends and family. There was Phillip, my patient who had died from AIDS, gaunt, spectral, gasping for breath as he whispered words I could not hear. Then, my grandmother, Lena Schwartz, dressed in black, her silver hair streaming over her shoulders, searching around my bedside, rooting around, looking and mumbling to herself. "What do you want, Grossmutter?" I try to ask her, but she cannot hear and goes on searching. Then, my father joins her. I see the back of his head as he kneels beside the mattress, looking for the lost treasure. His hair curls in a chalky ridge waving along the hairline, just like hers, just like mine. He is sorry, he tells me, because he has forgotten my birthday. He assures me that he didn't mean to, but he didn't realize what day it was. I reach for him to tell him that I understand and that he shouldn't worry, but just as I am about to touch him, he disappears.

Later that morning, after I had shaken off the fog of dreams, I poured a cup of dark French roast and curled up into an overstuffed chair, where I can brood over the churning waters of Puget Sound. The phone rang. My Aunt Gladys and Uncle Hugh have called to wish me a happy birthday and tell me stories—about my cousins, my ancestors who fought in the Civil War and about my father and mother as young parents. I began to cry, not only because my father wouldn't remember to call as he had every morning for fifty-two years, but because my mother probably wouldn't either as she, too, was becoming more forgetful. My aunt and uncle were surprised by my tears and fell silent for a moment, uncertain as to how to console me. They do their best, telling me how much my parents loved me.

As the first child, I've had a privileged position, knowing my parents and their siblings as young people. I've been alone with my parents when they were as young and happy together as they ever were. Perhaps that explains the sadness I always feel when I think of them now, realizing what they have lost, how they have become estranged, full of petty punishments and taunts. In the past, when they called me on my birthday, each in turn recalled the events of my birth, the awakening on an October morning, the ride to the factory while my mother waited in the car, then the quick trip to the hospital and my immediate appearance. How delighted they were! "Oh, everyone loved you!" they always told me, and yes, they loved each other then, too.

Later in the afternoon, I walked along the rocky shore of Puget Sound with Betty and our dog, Tasha. I hold her hand tightly as we skip along the stony shore, trying to avoid stumbling over the rugged outcroppings of tree trunks and lichen-covered shells. Whatever the future holds for us, I am determined to avoid following the path of my parents' lives together. There must be a way to love without inflicting injury and pain. There must be.

****

Dennis:

In the years after the anniversary party, known as Dad's "adjustment to retirement" period, he would come in and out of reality, suddenly having these little unexpected moments of clarity. I always drove with him to call on customers, most of them long time clients, and he was never an embarrassment. He was well-liked everywhere—John Christofferson, Eddie McKay, Ron Keller—they all were glad to see him. The old guys remembered him as a straightshooter with a big smile and

Mehr

a strong handshake who would make an honest deal without trying to cheat them. After forty years in this town of "Okies" and "Arkies," Dad knew everybody and his reputation was as good as gold.

When he couldn't drive and I didn't have time to offer him a lift, I felt helpless knowing that he was just sitting in that little office beside the shop. He had a lot of friends and needed to be active, but sometimes I had to work and couldn't just be his buddy. There was no point in suggesting a hobby because he had never learned to golf or enjoy hobbies—only work—and now this shop on Florence Avenue was the only place he felt he belonged.

I'm like him in some ways—hot tempered, or at least I was—somewhat insecure, and used a joke to cover it up. He was an insecure guy, too, underneath his big bravado and could be triggered into anger very easily. If you crossed him, just approached the line, he would strike like a snake. I tried to be careful with him whenever I could.

Still, I loved him and tried to make him feel useful. I often looked back at the White House, where he sat and rocked, looking though old papers, and wondered what else I could do.

I had to run a business, I had my own family to look after and there he sat—rock, rock, rock. Once, he made the statement that cut deeper than the rest. "This is no life," he said as he sat in his chair looking out the door. *Goddamit, another load of guilt on for not doing something about this...What am I supposed to do?*

I had no answer.

There were all those times that I picked up Big Al, as the guys at the shop now called him, when he got lost or had an accident. They don't really matter because at least I knew where he was. I couldn't lock him up in that little office all day, though. *What am I supposed to do?*

He was just so bewildered these days—an old white-haired man dressed up in his uniform, white short-sleeved shirt and blue cotton pants, ready to go to work, sitting in the office behind his store, waiting, waiting for what? I don't know and I couldn't make it better. It was all I could do to see him sitting there, listening to the damned radio, sorting papers over and over again, waiting for a phone that never rang. Why hadn't he learned to play golf?

Mehr

****

<u>Marilyn:</u>

Whenever I talked to my family, we would quickly dispense with the news of our lives and focus on "what to do about Dad." We needed some relief and it came from a most unlikely source. As an atheist, I don't believe in magical explanations for unlikely events, nothing in the universe can or will guide me to choose the right lottery number or avoid an accident. Even so, there have been these odd surprises and coincidences that have almost made me believe that a kindly presence was at work. When my mother's telephone rang in the middle of a Saturday lunch, she was unprepared for the caller.

"Hi, Mum. This is Graciela Broitman, your foreign exchange student. Guess what? I'm in New York."

Mother was too startled to understand. "What? Who? Could you repeat what you just said?"

"Mum, this is Gracie. Do you remember me? Gracie from Argentina? I was your foreign exchange student in 1961."

Mother paused as she incorporated the message. "Gracie, is this you? I can't believe it. Where are you?"

"New York. I'm working for the United Nations. I looked up your number hoping I would find you...Mum, Mum, are you there?

She was crying and laughing at once. "Yes, Gracie. I am here. Do you know that Marilyn is in New York? She'll want to see you. We *all* want to see you. Oh, Gracie, what a nice surprise!"

****

Judy:

Mother called me in Texas so exuberant she could hardly speak. "Judy, guess what? Gracie called me. She's in New York and wants to visit. Can you come?"

"Hold on, Mom. Let me get this right."

Graciela Noemi Bazet-White has always held a special place in our family. She came into our lives from Argentina during the late summer of 1961. Dark hair, ivory skin and 4'8" tall, she looked like a doll and we treated her like one. Dad had thought that all Spanish-speakers were Mexicans, immigrants who could not or would not learn English, so when he met Gracie, his prejudices were demolished. He was completely charmed. She was so small and delicate, the child-woman his other daughters had ceased to be. He teased her and brought her little gifts, basking in her wide-eyed response and instant warmth. Dad lived up to her expectations—the doting, loving American father *who never blew up or got angry.*

She saw us as the "ideal American family," and loved the way that Mom and Dad would hug and kiss each other in front of us. Unlike the typical American teenager, she enjoyed being with her adoptive parents, accompanying them on weekend trips and outings, always eager to discover something new about them and their vast new country.

I, too, found a comrade and soulmate in Gracie, a sister I never had. She was warm, open, uncritical, ready to share whatever she had without a quarrel or battle. We would often stay up late after we had finished our homework, talking and laughing, sharing feelings about boyfriends and dreams about the future. When she left at the end of the school year, we promised to write and always stay close and for awhile, we did write and Dad even visited her and the family in the late 60's, but then our letters were returned. We speculated that she had moved and worried that she may have been harmed during the military reign in Argentina. At last, she had returned. We all agreed to meet within a week in Los Angeles.

****

<u>Marilyn:</u>

Betty and I had just arrived in New York for a visit when the phone rang in Aunt Rose's apartment in Stuyvesant Town. A shiver of apprehension traveled up my spine as I ran to the kitchen to answer "the call from your mother." Was this the news of another fall? A medication reaction? A full-blown stroke? Whatever it was, I was prepared for bad news.

"You'll never guess what?" Mother whispered breathlessly into the phone. Without waiting for a reply, she went on. "Gracie, she just called me from New York. She's staying at Tudor City, working for the U.N...you *have* to see her."

I didn't need convincing. Within twenty minutes I had caught the First Avenue bus to the 49th Street stop where Gracie stood, all 4'8" of her, beside the entrance to the UN. We yelled and screamed in two languages, embraced and danced in front of all the multi-colored flags, then found a Greek coffee shop where we talked for hours, filling in, making notes, planning for the visit that she and her husband Marcelo would make to the family home in Hollydale.

Our spirits were so high that I was reluctant to tell her about Dad, but she had to know. I explained that sometimes he recognized us, but not always, and that he often had trouble expressing himself. He spoke a slurred kind of speech that only Mother could interpret. Gracie's big dark eyes clouded as tears ran down her cheeks. She reached out her hand and said, "Oh, Marilyn, I am so sorry." Then, I cried, too.

We all cried when we got together in Los Angeles two weeks later, crying for the happiness of reunion, the sadness of lost time. We laughed a lot, as well, sharing photographs and memories as we welcomed back a sister into the circle of family. Her memories of Dad helped us to recall the energy and vitality he brought into a room. We had begun to forget the man with the loud laugh and the big embrace, but when Gracie arrived, we remembered. We loved the man who was with us, but he seemed almost a benign spirit, listening, smiling, sleeping, but rarely speaking, except to say from time to time, "Gracie, is that you?"

***

CHAPTER EIGHT

MR. POTTER AND THE NIGHT CLERK (3/9/91)

> 2/7/91 Rancho: wt. 186 lbs. Marked decline in cognitive function. Fell 2 wks ago. Problems with dressing, can't handle buttons. No driving. Gets lost walking.
>
> This 80-year old right-handed gentleman returns for follow-up of dementia. He has been a patient at Rancho Los Amigos since 1985. His mental status scores have gradually declined from about 20 in 1985 to 18 in 1989 and to 10 during the past year.
>
> There was difficulty in repetition and concentration. He is unable to count backwards from 20. He was cooperative and had good effort but yawned on two occasions. For the most part his face seemed masked, but occasionally he breaks into a hearty laugh. Wife wants to know whether to take him to Texas to granddaughter's wedding. I agreed, but cautioned that he should never be left alone.
>
> H. Choi, M.D.

Mehr

Marilyn:

The four of us tried to help our parents with phone calls, money management, emotional support. At the same time, we had obligations to family, friends and work that also demanded our energy and attention. We visited Mother and Dad, but hadn't all gathered together as a family since their anniversary. It was painful to watch Dad spill food all over the table, his hands shaking so hard that he could hardly feed himself. So we went alone and watched Mother grimace and titter as Dad struggled to say an abbreviated blessing. We visited, but individually, unable to summon the will to draw everyone back into the family house.

When Judy's second daughter Karin announced her forthcoming marriage, we all welcomed a happy occasion that we could celebrate together. At least the three of us—myself, Nancy and Judy—could help Mother with Dad, so they could both adapt to the stress of travel. I was eager to get away from Washington for a few days, not only to escape the pressures of writing deadlines, but to get together with my family for a reason other than to commiserate with Mother over Dad's decline. Everyone could enjoy the wedding.

I arrived in Dallas twenty-four hours early, allowing myself time to explore, take the local buses, visit the art museum. The desk clerk seemed surprised when I asked for directions to the local bus stop. "Why," the clean-shaven young man exclaimed, "we've never had anyone ask us that before!" They referred the question to the black receptionist who knew exactly which bus to take and what it would cost me.

My day at the Dallas Art Museum became an adventure, a time to explore, see new paintings, eat lunch in the museum dining room and sit by the fountain watching the buses unload bunches of school kids, book bags flapping, pinching and squeezing as they lined up at the entrance. It was a splendid day and I returned just in time for a 20-minute nap which was cut short by the grating sound of car doors being slammed, footsteps in the hall, voices calling out in nasal Texas accents. Slipping on my shoes, I ran my hands through my hair and opened the door to greet them. At the end of the hallway was a middle-aged woman helping a very old man through the doorway. She braced herself against the door in order to ease him through. He shuffled as he walked, leaning on her as if they were contestants in a three-legged race. As they approached me, I recognized the couple as my sister Nancy and my Father.

His glasses were covered with a steamy film from his own exertions. *He doesn't recognize me because he can't see me,* I tell myself. Nonetheless, I called out to him, "Dad," and ran the remaining distance to him, embracing him as tightly as I could, feeling his skeleton through his clothes, smelling the sour odor of urine.

"Hey, Dad, it's Marilyn. How're you doing?"

He looked over my shoulder, then focused on my face. "All right," he says carefully. "What are *you* doing here?"

Nancy repeated a phrase she must have used a dozen times today. "Dad, Karin's getting married."

"Oh, yeah, that's it," he commented, pretending to remember.

His hands shook as the two of us led him toward the room we'll all be sharing. *Well, at least he knows me,* I told myself, craving the slight glimmer in his eyes that signaled recognition. In the last six months, though, he had become more precarious, bent like a question mark, trembling and shaking, constantly losing his balance. I knew how to read these markers. I understood fully that the shuffling, stooping and weight loss meant that the brain was shrinking and dying. The stocky, muscular German who always wore an "Extra Large" shirt to cover a body tightened and sinewed by endless summers of raking hay and riding horses, was now this slight, curved little figure, denuded like a bird that had moulted its feathers, exposing its fragile skeleton.

My mother appeared in the doorway, carrying several small paper sacks of items she had collected from the airlines. She has always been a collector of detritus, stuffing file cabinets with newspaper clippings, dresser drawers with worn-out pajamas, socks, plaques won by her children, class rings, Girl Scout pins—markers of family life, reminders of a fullness she once enjoyed. Now, she seems compelled to hold on to remnants, unable to return paper napkins to Southwest Airlines, unable to throw away a tuna sandwich she had packed in Los Angeles. Not only her home, but her person is loaded with paraphernalia. In spite of this compulsion to surround herself with objects and memorabilia, my father was leaving her, step by inevitable step toward the grave he would rest in alone. Passive in the face of larger forces, she had submitted most of her life to others, but was now adamant in her determination to hold on. She would document every event, hoard every letter, financial statement, newspaper and church program that she had received for the past fifty years. The Hollydale house resembled a museum in serious need of an archivist.

Following her into the small motel room were my niece and her fiance, Karin and Robert, full of optimism and expectation. The groom was slight with deep-set eyes and a wide Irish forehead. When he shook my hand, I felt the moisture on his palms and realize how frightened he must be at the reality of taking on so much family. I remembered that he is said to be a good cook, a sign that he will take care of my niece well. After a few jovial exchanges, they leave, promising to see us at dinner.

I invited my father for a cup of coffee in the hotel dining room. His eyes brightened and my mother tossed him a sweater in thankful parting. She looked tired, although she denied needing rest. Fatigue had become like an old friend, following her from room to room. Dad and I walked slowly together along one of many hallways leading to the coffeeshop. I held his arm and told him again where he was and why. His puzzlement was apparent, "Marriage," he repeats slowly, "what do they want to do *that* for?" *Some cells were working,* I told myself.

We found a seat in a booth distant from the clamor of the cash register and opened our menus. He stared at the brightly colored pictures and the brief descriptions of their pleasures, only pretending to read. I scanned the desserts, looking for a light snack: "Kahlua cream cheese pie, carrot cake with pineapple frosting, chocolate devil dreamcake, bourbon bread pudding." It is obvious that we are in a Southern kitchen. When the waitress arrived, I persuaded her to find a breakfast muffin which brought an instant smile to my father's face. He stirred his coffee, poured two thimblefuls of cream and three packets of sugar into his cup and stirred away. Shakily, he lifted a spoonful to his lips and smiled. It was right.

He should smile, I told myself, *he just made himself a hot milkshake.* When the muffin arrived, bloated with a dense mixture of bran, nuts. molasses and raisins, he breaks it apart gingerly into tiny mounds formed into an exact grid upon his plate. *What is he thinking?* I wondered as I watched this exercize in organization. Then, he began to eat, consuming each stack of muffin as he proceeds up each of five rows.

"Where are you living now?" he asked, in between bites. He seemed totally unaware of my curiosity about his behavior. *Will he change rows? Start at the top of the row? Choose from the middle?* Never. He selected from the bottom left-hand row and moved up. His actions were deliberate and without reflection, like a simple machine.

"Seattle," I repeat as I have for the past six months when we have spoken by telephone.

"Oh," he said, adding more butter to his muffin, "way up there."

I explained once more that I am writing a book. I told him that I was enjoying myself immensely, writing under the eaves of an upstairs attic overlooking Puget Sound and the Cascades. Then, in one of those rare moments of lucidity during this crowded weekend, he looked directly at me and asked, "Well, do you keep a schedule?"

BROKEN CIRCUITS
A Memoir of Alzheimer's Disease in Four Voices

Desperate to engage him in a real conversation, I explained that I write in the morning, have lunch, then write in the afternoon. "Yes, Dad, a schedule helps," I say, hoping that we have embarked on a conversation.

"Yes, I thought so," and once again his eyes became dull and void, as though an electric switch had been thrown, cutting off all current to his brain. He had no further thoughts, no questions about the life of this daughter, the one he held in his arms and nicknamed "Pumpkin," the one whose features mimicked his—the high, square forehead, wide lips, dark hair, olive skin, the one who called him "Daddy-Boy," and heard his friends exclaim, "Al, as long as she's alive, you'll never die!"

He felt none of the primitive connection to his offspring, no anxiety to protect, no feelings of pride, anger, hurt or disappointment. For now, there is nothing. His face is flat and unresponsive, the only urge remaining is to taste and chew. When the waitress passed our table, he pointed to his empty cup as though a gesture would fill it. For a moment, there was no response, so he looked into the distance and yelled, "Hey!" at a passing figure. Trying to suppress a rush of embarrassment, I smiled sheepishly at her and asked apologetically for a refill, feeling ashamed as though my dog had just barked. This feeling of shame and anger brought sharp memories of his rough treatment of others. *How uncouth my father could be, never trying to polish his presentation, always relying on the skills learned in the workplace, the rough speech of men talking to men.*

"Dad, it's all right," I cautioned him. "I'll call her. Don't yell."

And I did, in the cultured, modulated voice I have perfected through the years of college and postgraduate training that his money purchased, the money that allowed me to enter a world of sophisticated and well-mannered people who have no awareness of the uncultivated earth of my childhood. I felt a sudden rush of anger over his clumsiness. *He knows better,* I told myself, *why does he act like such an oaf?* I glanced out the window at the arriving guests and decided that this roughness is just who he is. Any other behavior would be pretense.

We drank more coffee. I paid the check and helped him stand up. Even though he shuffled, he offered me his arm, a courtly gesture that made me want to weep. *Not yet,* I tell myself, *do not cry now. There will be plenty of time, later.* He held my hand, pressing my arm tightly to his body as though I might shy away or get lost, enfolding my hand in his with a tender pat. As we walked together past the gift shop along the narrow hallway to our room, father and daughter in a small promenade, I was sure that he could not tell me my name.

****

Judy:

With all the calls, orders and schedules to manage for a wedding, I felt like a dispatcher at United Parcel rather than the mother of the bride. My family, Jim's family, our family were all gathering in Dallas to celebrate the marriage of Karin, our second daughter, to Robert Williams, a fellow medical student at Baylor. Jim and I were delighted.

I planned the wedding, organizing invitations, motel reservations, a pre-wedding banquet and a reception. We would all meet in Dallas, near the LDS Temple, at a motel, have dinner, sleep overnight, and arrive at the temple early in the morning for the wedding ceremony. Then, we would drive to our hometown of Huntsville for a reception.

Mehr

I worried that I wouldn't be able to support Mom in caring for Dad, so I was relieved when Nance called to say that she would fly to California, then fly to Texas to accompany them. Marilyn would meet us in Dallas and could also help care for Dad who would likely be disoriented by the trip. He was somewhat weak and forgetful, but still essentially himself, and had expressed a desire to attend the wedding. *Why not,* I thought to myself, *even if I still feel resentment toward him, he is, after all, Karin's grandfather.*

At the dinner on Friday evening, the bride and groom were surrounded by about thirty friends and relatives and seemed so in love, touching and hugging, laughing easily with each other. Afterwards, we all went to our rooms. Jim, Brad, and I had exchanged rooms with our friends, the Potters, so that the bride and bridesmaids could stay in adjoining rooms. Karin would be wearing the dress and veil I had worn at my own wedding, on July 31, 1965, and we had practiced setting the veil over her head to keep her hair curled in tendrils around her face. She agreed to knock on my door at 4:30 the next morning to help her get dressed before the ceremony.

BROKEN CIRCUITS
A Memoir of Alzheimer's Disease in Four Voices

I ruminated about every detail of her appearance until I finally fell into a sound sleep. A loud rapping on the door startled me into consciousness. The digital clock beside the bed glimmered 2:00 a.m. and I stumbled to the door where, to my surprise, a hotel security guard stood beside my father who was naked from the waist down. The man asked if my name were "Potter" because my father insisted that his name was "Potter." Dad had been wandering the hallways of the motel in the top half of his pajamas, telling everyone that his name was "Potter," so of course, the security guard brought him to the Potter's room. Looking embarrassed and confused, Dad held his hand in front of his genitals. I thanked the guard, wrapped Jim's robe around my father, and walked with him down the hallway, both of us dazed and mute. When we reached the room where my mother and two sisters were sleeping, I rapped on the door, explained to Mother what had happened and passed Dad over to her.

When I returned to my own darkened cubicle, I slipped under the covers beside Jim and tried to remain still. The images of my naked father stooped over in the hallway holding his genitals and mumbling, "Potter," kept merging in my mind

Mehr

with those of my sweet daughter dressed in my heirloom gown. I started to cry softly, so as not to bother anyone. Soon, my quiet tears turned to hysterical sobs and gulps of air as I tried to explain to Jim what had just happened. Half out of my head with sorrow, whirling into a mini-nervous breakdown, I pleaded, "Promise me, promise me! Promise me that you will kill me if I ever get like that! Kill me! Kill me! Kill me!"

In the middle of my outburst, my eleven year-old son awakened in astonishment and terror. *Was this some kind of weird nightmare?* he must have wondered. Jim kept his voice low, telling Brad that his mother was okay and that he should go back to sleep, then he held me closely, rocking me and reassuring me that he wouldn't kill me, but promised to take care of me, if I lost it and became demented. I don't know whether he will, but he talked me down, said the right words and allowed me to sleep for another hour.

When I heard Karin's faint knock on the door at 4:30, I realized that this mother-of-the-bride had undergone far too much "Sunrise/Sunset" for a sparkling presentation. I got up, put on a robe and stuffed all my feelings of terror and madness into some private place and attended to the needs of my daughter Karin, the beautiful bride in her mother's wedding dress. I needed to focus on the sunrise, arrange her train and veil, smile for the pictures, shake hands with friends, exchange hugs in a receiving line and forget last night, for the moment. A very tall order!

Dad didn't make it for the wedding ceremony. The morning's disaster had been equally upsetting for him. After I left him, he threw up and was ill for the rest of the morning. Marilyn stayed with him at the motel while Nancy brought Mother to the Temple. We were all there together later for the pictures, but I kept seeing my own "photo" of my father and the security guard as the image ran through my head like a silent movie, my father running frenetically through the hallways, like a comedian in a silent film, pitching to and fro as he quietly slams himself against the walls of the Nowhere Hotel.

After the ceremonies were over, we tried to settle in for a "normal" night's sleep, but Dad wandered again, this time falling down the stairs of our home and cutting his head. We always left the hall light on, but Mom had insisted that it was wasteful and had turned it off. *Did she want these accidents to happen?* I could hardly allow myself to ask the question, but she seemed to want to draw attention to him. It was hard for me to admit that her lapses in caring for him could have been intentional. Did she actually enjoy having helicopters circle the sky looking for him, having the hospital call and say he had crashed his car into a brick wall, or having her daughter escort him down the hallway of a motel half-naked? If she didn't, she would secure the locks and take his keys away, something she still refused to do.

I allowed myself to ask these dark questions but not to arrive at any conclusions. Was my mother really Lady MacBeth in disguise? Someone I had thought was the victim who could now be the perpetrator? I felt like I was going nuts, so I did what I always do when I'm churning, I started cooking. I baked a big sponge cake with yellow icing and we all sang, "Happy Birthday" which made him laugh and ask, "What are you doing?"

I said, "Dad, we're celebrating your 80th birthday!" He laughed again, as though I had just told him he had grown a third leg, and said, "I'm not 80!" Marilyn asked him how old he was. He smiled, licking the frosting from his fingers, and said, "Oh, around 60."

I've remembered the events surrounding Karin's wedding many times since then, mostly with revulsion and horror. I think for me, the dad I had known since childhood died that weekend. I didn't grieve his loss, I just turned away to my own family. I had a dear husband and four wonderful children who loved and needed me. It was their love that preserved me and I couldn't get caught in the sidewinder of my father's decline.

Jim always tells me, "You know, you are a strong, capable, independent woman in our home. When you get around your family you become emotional and weak, in fact, kind of nutty." I had known two homes in my life, the one where I now lived and felt good about myself and this other one in Hollydale, California, where my father was dying, little by little, and I felt helpless. He was disappearing by inches. We all pretended, but I knew I no longer had a father. *There was this person in a motel hallway who thought his name was "Potter" and he's a nice person who deserves kindness because he's old. Sure, he's a man, whatever, but he wasn't my father.*

Mehr

He wasn't going to say, "Hey, how're you doing, Snuggy?" That person was gone.

****

<u>Nancy:</u>

I was exhausted after the wedding, but we still had a three-hour drive to Huntsville for the reception. Mother, Dad, Marilyn and I drove from Dallas to Huntsville, sleeping, conversing about the scenery, avoiding any talk about Dad's midnight wandering. We drank some punch and wished the bride and groom a happy life, then finally returned to Judy's and went to bed.

Mom and Dad slept upstairs where Mom had placed her mattress across the door to prevent Dad from wandering in the night. One evening in the funhouse was enough! Someone had left a light on upstairs, but I was still worried that Dad might awaken and become confused. The next thing I heard was Dad crashing down the stairs. He rolled to the floor and was moaning in pain as I jumped up, rushing to his side. My astonishment in that moment was in realizing just how much love I felt for him. He was so helpless and vulnerable, unable to understand where he was or what had happened.

Mother appeared, we checked for broken bones, bandaged up his abrasions and all went back to bed once again. As I tried to sleep, I remembered watching Jack Lemmon in the movie, "Dad," how he stumbled and lost his bearings in the dark, just as Dad had done. Then, I realized how dark it must have seemed for Dad. I understood that when he would insist he wasn't home—when he was—he must have remembered the house as it was thirty years ago.

Then, I remembered being in that house thirty years ago, for my "Sweet Sixteen Dinner," when we were all sitting around the kitchen table. The phone rang. Dad answered and made some "wise" remark as he gave the phone to me. When I jokingly tapped him on the head as I left the table, he was so insulted that he grabbed the phone and threw it at me as I ran through the living room, tripping over Judy's little rocking chair. I scrambled across the carpet on all fours to my room, slammed the door in defiance of his threats and started to cry. When I could finally stop, I started shouting epithets at him—

"Damned stupid fool, I hate you" piercing the walls and, I hoped, his heart.

In the middle of my outburst, he opened the door, sat down beside me on my bed and apologized. I was so shocked I could only ask him, "Why?" Why could he change from laughter to anger in a second without any warning? Maybe I made him feel like a fool. Yes, and there I go blaming myself for his behavior. He was at fault, not me!

Anyway, Dad had crashed to the floor in my sister's house to cap the events of a truly horrible day. In spite of myself, I felt guilty and wished I could have prevented his fall. I also felt real love for him that night. All the rancor and resentment of past misunderstandings left me as I helped him back up the stairs. This was a man terribly flawed, but terribly human. This was a man who had taken his last trip.

****

Marilyn:

Nancy and I sat beside Dad at the wedding party dinner gently reminding him of his purpose and location. When the waiter brought him a Texas-sized slab of prime rib, his eyes lit up and he reached across the table for a bottle of Thousand Island dressing. Before we could stop him, he poured the dressing all over the meat like a frothy pink glaze. He seemed to enjoy his horrible concoction, so we chopped up his meat and let him eat in peace.

Everyone socialized for awhile, then Mother and Dad soon departed with most of the guests and returned to their room. I wasn't sleepy, so I lingered over my coffee, relishing a few moments to talk with my brother-in-law, Jim, about his latest book, a biography of John Wayne. We had radically different opinions about the man, so we argued, listened, considered, then debated and realized that we were still far apart on our views. Jim tried to convince me that JW was more than a chauvinist/sexist/cowboy, but I remained unconvinced. We both enjoyed the argument.

When I returned to the hotel room I realized that I had checked into a dormitory room for adults—Mom and Dad in one bed, Nance and I in another. All three were snoring when I slipped beneath the covers. For hours, it seemed, I tried to figure out a cadence which would lull me to sleep, and I couldn't. First one began a minuet, then the next a little pirouette, then the next a 2/2 march, then on to another sequence of jagged fits and starts. I measured the breathing of those two who gave me life, who protected and loved me. interrupted by my second sister who sleeps a disrupted slumber, gasping for breath, coughing out spasms of air. At times, I thought I was going cuckoo and even wished for it, just a few moments of a dissociative state when I could believe I was Princess Marie of Romania asleep on a bed of leaves in the forests, but at last I drifted away for a small respite.

Not to last, this delicate peace. Knock, knock, knock...*was it Banquo's ghost?* No, standing there before me were my sister-in-tears, and my father-sans-culottes, beside a bewildered security guard. My mother took charge, dragged my Father back into the room and began to berate him for his behavior. "Where were you, Al? How did you get out? What do you mean, you couldn't find the right room?" Nance and I kept a shameful silence. I wished I were anywhere in the world but in this room.

"Mother, let him go to bed," I finally called to her. "Can't you see he doesn't know the answer to your questions?

If he knew the answers, he wouldn't be wandering the damned hallways with no clothes on!"

She was silent and I worried that she was crying. Not to worry, she was planning her retort. "Al, why did you tell them your name was Potter?"

"Because it is!" he yelled in one final outburst.

I started to laugh and my sister joined in until the bed shook with our stifled giggles, bursts of shame, anger and disbelief. We all felt guilty, but none of us has done anything wrong. This man who ran a million dollar business, who drove his employees ruthlessly, cajoling and threatening like a drill sergeant, who knew every mechanic in his Grapes of Wrath community by name, called out to most of them as they walked up to the counter of Mehr Auto Parts could now not even remember his own name.

Of course, the laughter turned to tears. My sister and I, at last, wept softly until we slept.

In the morning, we three women took turns using the bathroom. Dad was still dazed and groggy, sitting on the edge of the bed, when all at once, he began to hold his sides and moan. Nancy and I became a complete Emergency Room team as I ran into the bathroom, pushing Mother aside, as Nancy lept across the bed, lifting him to his feet and pressing him toward the open bathroom door where I met him and guided him to the toilet. He retched over and over again, giving up the airline cannelloni, giving up a bran muffin, giving up a huge cut of prime rib covered with Thousand Island dressing. Finally, he was finished. My sister and I wiped him off with damp towels and helped him back to bed where he returned to an untroubled sleep.

Insisting that my sister and mother go to the wedding, I reassured them that I could help Dad to get dressed and would meet them later. "Don't worry about us. We'll be fine. Just go," I admonished them. When they left, I ordered tea, read the paper and begin to awake him. He sits up, sips some of the hot liquid, listens with a curious expression on his face as I tell he has been sick and should take a bath. Like a child, he follows me to the bathroom where I have drawn a steaming tub of water whose thermal values, I hope, will restore some integrity to his person.

I had never undressed my father. As a child, I saw him leave the bathroom, but always wrapped in a towel. An old taboo restrained me now, as I looked at his withered body. *He needs help and he needs to be clean.*, I told myself, so I try to imagine being his nurse. Then, very professionally, I removed his pajama tops. "Come on, Big Al, it's time for a bath." I said, realizing that he felt no inhibitions as he allowed me to remove his shirt, then his pants. He stepped into the steaming water and, as he settled, he suddenly became embarassed, lifting a wash cloth from the side of the tub to cover his genitals and smiling shyly. He was, after all, in the presence of his daughter.

I washed his back, recalling the map of scars and moles I had not seen since childhood. In the long arid summers in Los Angeles, we would all retreat to the beach where Dad and I would dig sand castles, roasting sensuously in the summer sun. As I lathered his skin with soap, I see how small his once-broad shoulders have become, like the structure of a model airplane covered by a thin tissue of skin. His muscles were soft and flaccid, no longer sinewy and able to throw a frisbee across two neighborhood lots. I wash the tendrils of white hair crowning his skull and notice that the back of his head is almost flat, as though pressed by a hat too tight for his head. "Where have you gone, Joe DiMaggio?" I hum softly to myself. He hears me and smiles, blankly.

Gently, I help him to rise, dry off and dress. He drank a few sips of tea and flipped through the pages of the newspaper, an elderly gentleman in a white shirt and tie reviewing the day's events. How composed he appeared when my mother and sister arrived full of news of the wedding.

We hurried along with them in the stark Dallas sunlight, squinting at the rows of family members lined up for photographs on the steps of the Mormon temple. My Father and I stood beside them, dazed and disconnected from the group, almost like passers-by mustered into a family portrait.

I was worn out by this Walpurgis night of naked wandering and violent purging. With a long drive to Huntsville and an evening's wedding reception still ahead of us, I would be ill-prepared for still another crisis when Dad would carome down the Olson's stairs and land on his head. It was evident to all of us except Mother that Dad needed the safety and familiarity of his own home. If we could arrange for Mother to travel separately, she could escape for her own renewal and health. But for Dad, this was his last trip and we all knew it.

***

CHAPTER NINE

A TIME-OUT FOR MOTHER (1992)

> 5/16/92 Pt. doing well now. Sleeps a lot. No problems with eating. No driving. No headaches. Mental status 10/30. Some inappropriate comments suggestive of delusions or hallucinations, for example, he will say, "Oh damn that creature" with no apparent reason or speak about his mother, as though she were still alive. For the most part his face seems masked but occasionally he breaks into a hearty laugh.
>
> 6/11/92 MRI Scan: Generalized atrophy, especially of temporal lobe with dilation of ventricles and prominence of the sylvian fissure. A lacunar infarct seen in the right basal ganglion and some white matter ischemic changes.
>
> H. Choi, M.D.

Marilyn:

It was almost Thanksgiving, 1992, and Betty and I were back in our glass house in Los Angeles. As we poured our morning coffee, we could see the Tehachapi Mountains covered with a fresh layer of snow, and agreed that it was nice to be back in California. Betty was healthy and happy to return to her graduate students at U.S.C. and I had taken a position as Chair of Health Psychology at the California School of Professional Psychology. Our year in Washington provided us with a needed retreat, but we were both excited to be in L.A. again, with its multi-hued neighborhoods and open-faced citizens, even though it meant struggling through frenetic lanes of traffic. After a few months of working, we welcomed a weekend escape to a friend's cabin at Big Bear Lake. The owner, Eric Cohen, was off to Canada for a week, and had been generous as usual with his possessions.

Even though I found myself in a beautiful site, I still couldn't shake my concern over Dad. If I manage to forget about him for a while, I can then think about the owner of the cabin, Eric, who has just told us that he has AIDS. His presence in the cabin is manifest everywhere, in the many photos, wall hangings, souvenirs, even the notes for the use of appliances. "This is a Tutorial 101 for Appliance Dummies. I know you are not stupid, but I want you to keep reading because I do not want you to burnout my coffee pot or ruin my microwave. I do want you to enjoy them, so read this!" Eric will probably die soon, too young, too vulnerable to this creeping virus nibbling away at his blood cells. I'm beginning to feel that I can't escape the sour breeze of death, blowing through the trees, caressing my hair, calling out my name to remind me of its presence.

When I had visited my parents over the past few months, I expected to see my father's increasing signs of infirmity. Yet, sometimes, he would surprise me. According to family custom, we would gather around the dinner table waiting for a blessing to be said over the food. My father would now shuffle to his chair, gaze into space until Mother asked him to pray, then launch into an old family blessing, "Our Father in heaven, we are thankful for this food and ask you to bless it to our use. We are thankful for the hands that prepared it. In the name of Jesus Christ, Amen," Whatever damage had been done to his brain by Alzheimer's disease, there was still a protected storage vault containing that prayer.

Mehr

Eric would never have uttered such a blessing. He would have simply tapped his finger on the table and said, "Hey, Babe, let's eat!" *Why him?* I wondered as Betty and I drove down the mountain on Monday morning. *Why any of us?* Shortly after I met Eric, in 1976, at Children's' Hospital, he asked me to lunch at a Japanese restaurant and told me he was convinced that he would die young, just as his father. I was surprised that he shared such a personal belief and understood thereafter why he lived as intensely as he did. He was curious and adventuresome, wanting to meet unusual people, never afraid to take risks, even with strangers, even with sex. No one had heard of AIDS and no one in my age group had died, yet. Eric ate health foods and exercised daily; he could never be the first. Or so we thought.

I steered the Chevy Blazer toward the onramp of the San Bernardino Freeway trying to pay attention to Betty as she told me about her recent book-promotion tour. She had this laser-like ability to pinpoint hypocricy and pretense in people as she punctured the facade of various radio and television interviewers. Her commentary was a welcome distraction from my dark musings on death. I burst out laughing when she said, "Well, I told Kathie Lee that we all have choices, that Existentialism is everywhere!"

"You said that?" I asked incredulously, "Oh, that's wonderful!"

"Not only that, but..." Listening, I tried to enjoy her report, but I felt anxious and worried. I wondered how my folks were doing.

As soon as we unpacked, I called my mother. "Well, this has been a weekend," she began, her voice quivering with a mix of excitement and fear. "Patrol cars, helicopters, flyers spread around the neighborhood with your father's picture on them, "Missing, Al Mehr"...I didn't know he had gone." *Uh, huh, probably had a fight.* "He had walked the dog once and I told him not to go again..." *She's trying to handle the guilt. I've asked her to keep the front door locked and she won't do it. Does she want him "missing?"*

"...And then, he didn't come back. After an hour, I went looking for him, called the South Gate Police—they are really something, our boys in blue! Then, your brother came over, the Bishop, CiCi, our neighbor...she was crying, so worried...six hours later, at 11:00 o'clock, a squad car brings him home...the officer says he was found by a motorist under an overpass of the Long Beach Freeway, holding his dog and—I don't know what happened to the leash. The dog was so tired, he slept all day." *The dog,* I want to yell, *what about the husband, the father, the guy who got up every god-damned morning at 6:00 to sell auto parts all day, what about him?"* At this moment, I am sure she wants him dead.

"I asked him over and over again where he had been. All he can say is that he was going to Illinois. Isn't that silly?" Without waiting for my reply, she continues, "He must have meant Ohio, where you were born." *Yes, Mom, and why would he want to go back to where I was born?* "He has no idea where he has been...all these hours...who knows?"

Indeed. The alarm bells go off in my head in concert. Beneath the din, I try to think, to reconstruct what I have just heard. *He walks the dog at dusk, his worst time of day, does not return for six hours during which time helicopters have circled the neighborhood dropping flyers with his photograph plastered on them while he hides under an overpass! Meanwhile, she is worried about the dog leash?* I call my brother. This time something must change.

BROKEN CIRCUITS
A Memoir of Alzheimer's Disease in Four Voices

On Wednesday evening my brother and I joined my parents around the family table, passing dishes of cole slaw, carrots, pickled beets, roast chicken, talking about the weather, the neighbors, the dog. Finally, I cleared my throat and brought up the missing persons event.

"You know, Dad was lost for six hours...very dangerous, wandering around...could have been killed by a stranger, an automobile, a dog bite. No one wants that." I paused, waiting for confirmation. A few nods.

Then, Dennis, dear, sweet brother, told them how he felt. "Listen to me for a few minutes...what happened scared me to death. It probably scared you, too. Not only that, but I'm worried about your fighting. This is no way to spend your final time together and I can tell you one thing, I don't want to remember you this way."

Dad appeared to listen, and then very slowly, he spoke, slurring and whispering, telling us that he was scared, too. He began to cry, pushing his carrots around with his fork. I put my arm around his shoulder and then we both cried. My brother wipes his eyes and Mother got up to pour tea.

Mehr

We have held yet another family conference to cope with a crisis and found some measure of agreement. Mother will drive Dad to Adult Day Care twice a week and hire a boy to walk beside Dad on his afternoon "excursions" with the dog. Mother showed limited resolve, still expressing doubt that Dad would cooperate. My brother and I stood beside his Jaguar in the driveway as he prepared to leave and I expressed my admiration for the way he simply shared his feelings, refraining from pressuring or criticizing our parents, allowing them to feel respected and worthy even though they were both endangered by their mistakes. My appreciation touched him and he began to cry again. "Oh, Damn," he said, hugging me quickly before leaving.

"We've been a team again, you and me, kid," I call out to him, thinking about the times when we rode through the Rancho and shared a picnic under a eucalyptus tree. *Hey, bro, put this baseball cap on your head, that's it, and sit on the fender of the bicycle. Yeah, keep your feet away from the spokes and hold on, here, around my waist. Got it? Good. Now let's go.!*

BROKEN CIRCUITS
A Memoir of Alzheimer's Disease in Four Voices

****

Dennis:

What can I say? I don't have words for what I feel about all of this. My old man and his little dog hiding under a freeway overpass, hoping to get to Ohio, or if that failed, Indiana? This is not how a life should end, wandering around your own neighborhood unable to find your way home without a police escort. *Damn, damn, damn, what can I do?*

When the helicopters circled and the police passed out flyers with his photo on them, *what could I do?* The officers brought him home holding his little dog, Skippy, in a blanket, shaking and shivering. These guys looked at me like I was a criminal. *There's his son over there, the one who dropped him off on the freeway and sped away! What an ungrateful jerk!*

****

Marilyn:

We had to do something, but what? I wrote to my two sisters, even though I knew that they had heard about Dad's getting lost. Since Mother was still wavering about getting more help, I

Mehr

wanted both Nancy and Judy to convince her that she had to accept someone in her home part-time to care for Dad or she would get sick. She already looked worn out.

Dear Nance and Judy,   March 1, 1993

I scheduled a meeting last week with a social worker, Steve Barlam, whose specialty is geriatric case management. He asked to meet with Mom, Dad, me and our brother. I invited Den and he agreed to come, although I think that Mother told him that he didn't have to join us if it was too much trouble. He wasn't there and I'm not sure why. I've called Den since the meeting, but he hasn't yet answered. Do you see why we need a case manager?

    Anyhow, Steve was wonderful. He was patient, yet persistent, asking lots of good "social work" questions and promising to provide a written summary in a week's time with referrals and recommendations. In the meantime, he encouraged Mother to plan one visit per month to a location beyond L.A. where she could get some perspective and recharge her batteries. I have offered to plan a long weekend for starters. We will probably go to Las Vegas, a town I loathe, despise and detest, but I will enjoy seeing our Uncle Max and Aunt Marge, and so will she. The two of you could keep the ball rolling by inviting her for a week in either April or May. I have spoken to Ruben, the man referred to me by the Rancho program, and he is willing to stay with Dad on the weekend or longer, if necessary.

Of course, these are band-aids to a larger problem, but each application covers at least a scratch. When the summary arrives I will send you a copy so you have the same information that I do. I will also share it with our brother.

As Steve advised, "Leave the big picture alone for now. Just plan your first trip on your own. That will be enough." And how.

Let's keep talking.

Abrazos y Besos, Marilyn

P.S. I'm enclosing Steve's letter. He's absolutely right. Mother needs to escape, but will she do it?

Dear Mrs. Mehr,   February 28, 1993

Please excuse the delay in getting this letter to you. It was a pleasure to meet with you and your family two weeks ago. I have enclosed a list of services that may be helpful in managing the care of your husband.

From my varied experience with families, I realize how challenging it is at times to care for a spouse with Alzheimer's. It can feel like a never-ending responsibility. So often the well spouse focuses most of her energy and attention on her spouse without paying attention to her own needs. If you do not take care of yourself by taking adequate "time off," you may become ill and unable to care for your husband. For now, I suggest that you leave the big picture alone. Just plan your first trip. That will be enough.

Sincerely,

Steve Barlam, LCSW,

Senior Care Manager

A few days after the letter arrived, I met Mother for lunch at a local coffee shop close to the Santa Ana Freeway. The walls were decorated with murals depicting scenes from French music halls, women kicking their legs into the air in garish cartoon renditions of the can-can. Edith Piaf sang, "Johnny, tu n'es pas un ange," as my mother, looking tired and unkempt in a blue jogging suit, peered down the rows of booths to find me. She withdrew the letter from Steve from her handbag and tossed it on the table.

"Well, here's the word from the expert. How much did *this* cost you?"

"Mom, it's not the money, it's the message."

"So you say. I say the message isn't worth the money. Anybody could have come up with this advice. Sure. Take a vacation."

Her eyes dulled to a dull mossy green as she shrugged her shoulders and picked up the menu. She ordered a tuna-melt, something she could have made at home.

"Mom, you look tired. We can call Ruben. You and I can visit Uncle Max in Las Vegas. Wouldn't you like to see your brother and Aunt Margie?"

For a moment, her face brightened. I knew she would never travel just for the pleasure of it, but she take a trip if she could visit a relative, "tend to family business," as she said. Perhaps, she might even put a quarter in a slot machine.

"Maybe. I'm not agreeing to anything, yet. I know I have to take care of myself and maybe I could if he weren't so damned contrary."

"Mom, do you think he's faking this?"

"I wouldn't put it past him!" My hand shook as I picked up the check. I wanted to grab her neck and start shaking her until she admitted what had happened. The battle was over. She had won. *How much more evidence did she need?* He was pissing in his pants, falling down stairs and getting lost under freeway trestles. Couldn't she see how sick he had become? I had never exploded at my mother in my life and it didn't seem fair to unload on her now, but I wanted to, wanted to tell her how I angry I felt for all the needling and sarcasm she had leveled at him. I also wished she had stood up for herself whe he had jabbed at her, drew a line that declared, a line, "Enough was enough!"

I stood up and picked up my jacket. "Come on, Mom. I've got to get back to work. I have a patient at two o'clock."

She wrapped her sandwich in a napkin, mixing in a stack of limp french fries and the remains of a dill pickle.

Stuffing the package in her handbag, she smiled at me as I drummed my fingers on the table.

"This will be dinner for your father…a little soup, a few carrot sticks, and he'll be happy as a bear in winter. Of course, he eats anything, always has."

"Come on, Mom. I'm late."

****

<u>Judy:</u>

If Marilyn wanted me to invite my parents to Texas, I was having none of it. I had just finished fifty-two mid-term exams and looked forward to a week for myself, visiting my new granddaughter in Houston, seeing a few friends, enjoying a little time with my son Brad who was starring in the high school production of "H.M.S. Pinafore." Brad was so handsome in his white uniform that I wanted to cry when I saw him, so full of confidence, so talented. He sang, he danced, he knocked them dead! I would not share these moments with my parents. They were mine alone.

Mehr

A letter was another matter. At least, I could offer some support by writing and ease my conscience one more time. A few weeks after I received Marilyn's letter, I found some stationery laced with pansies and marigold and started to write:

Dear Mother, March 10, 1993
We all feel that Dad's last two falls are markers to consider moving into a more intense level of care for you and Dad. We realize that you have wanted to keep him comfortable in your home without much outside help. We also realize that this has worn you out physically and emotionally. If you could outline the way you want your life to be, given Dad's difficulties, what would you want? I think you would want members of the church to be more involved, but Dad's hygiene needs are very private.

Anyway, all of us feel that a social worker would be an excellent place for you to turn. Perhaps you could find someone who could live in the back room. He or she could care for the house as well as assist Dad with dressing and so on. If you didn't have to deal with the incontinence, you would have more resources for your own needs.

We love you and are hurting, too, as we see him decline and you as well. You have worked a lifetime to be able to guarantee a level of comfort for both of you IN YOUR OWN HOME. We'll help you cover the added expenses if this is a problem.

If you need a kind voice or a chat, we are not a moment away by phone. Together, we all love you and want you to have this help.

Love, Judy

****

Then, a few days later, I received a return letter from Mother. Her handwriting was shaky, almost illegible. The paper was stained and torn.

Dear Judy,   March 20, 1993

Thanks for your letter. Everyone feels that I should get away for awhile, but when I do, I just keep wondering how Dad's doing. I always worry. I suppose I can never get away from that. It's a fact of life, this worrying, even though it's a relief, just for your body to escape the constant overseeing.

    I'll try, tho.

Love, Mom

P.S. Today's your Dad's 82nd birthday. Of course, he doesn't know it, but I'll bake him a cake anyway. He'll always love sweets.

<u>Marilyn:</u>
My sisters hadn't telegrammed an invitation to Mother to visit. I knew that they were busy, but they couldn't see the damage that was being done to Mother's health by her constant caregiving. I insisted that we take a trip together. When I arrived, Mother seemed to be tied to a centrifugal force buried beneath the floor of the house. She would go to her bedroom, search for a piece of clothing, return to the brown leather recliner where Dad slept, looking dazed and disoriented; she would then wander to the kitchen, wrap some fruit in a paper bag, then return to ground zero again; she then went to the bathroom, combed her hair, looked for her lipstick, and came

back to Dad to cover him with his bathrobe. Finally, I took her arm and guided her towards the car.

"Mom, he'll be fine. Ruben is here. He will call if there is a problem. Don't worry." At last, she followed me to the car, folded herself into the front seat of my Mazda and fastened the seat belt for the trip to Las Vegas. Soon, we were on the highway, talking, remembering other trips, listening to music, admiring the desert in the full bloom of springtime. Did she stop worrying? Not for a minute, but she allowed herself three full days away.

Mother's oldest brother Max and his wife Aunt Marge met us in the doorway of their adobe-colored house at the foothills of the mountains. Mother joined in immediately, helping Marge cook, reminding Max of childhood friends and events. She hardly noticed when I left on Saturday evening with a friend, a professor at the University of Nevada, for a dinner at one of the local hot spots. I walked down the driveway with Brad without a worry. Mother was actually enjoying herself.

All the way home, we recalled small events of the weekend. It was working, this respite, I told myself. *One little*

Mehr

success. Perhaps she will do it again, even once a month, who knows? As we pulled into the driveway of their home late in the afternoon, our escape came to an abrupt end when we discovered my father sitting on a chair in front of the open garage. On the concrete facing, my brother Dennis was riding a wheelchair in circles like a six-year old at a birthday party. *What was he doing here? And where was Ruben?* I would soon find out.

****

<u>Dennis:</u>

Marilyn remembered coming home with Mom to find the two of us in the driveway—Sure, I would rather have been somewhere else, but I'm glad that I was close enough to come *home* to take care of my father when he needed me. I knew that Mother and Marilyn had gone to Las Vegas to give Mom a "time-out," and that Ruben would be staying at the house with Dad. My phone rang on Sunday morning, awakening me from a deep sleep. It was Louise, my parents' next door neighbor, calling to say that Ruben has just left—a family emergency, or God knows what—and my father was alone in the house.

I'm glad she found me because I think, even though it may have been a little one-sided, that that was one of our best visits. We laughed, went for a drive, bought a few beers, talked about old times. Here I was, a forty-six year old son doing wheelies in the driveway with an open beer while my Dad cheered me on. He smiled, *really smiled*, at me that day.

Bye, Dad.

****

<u>Marilyn:</u>

My first trip alone with Mother had taught us all two valuable lessons, one being that we could not rely on any one person to take care of him, the second that Mother could actually get away for a weekend and enjoy herself. I began to search for a facility that would allow short-term stays. One of the social workers at The Rancho had said her clients had been happy with Brittany House, in the nearby suburb of Bellflower. It was close, so Mother and I spent an afternoon visiting the staff and making a reservation for Dad to stay for four days in September. Mother could attend Nancy's son's wedding and get some rest as well.

Mehr

Dad could have stayed with either one of us, my brother or myself, but we worked full-time jobs and both had full-time mates who were protective of our time. In fact, we could have stayed with Dad at the house. Somehow, I didn't think it was fair. If we could afford to make him comfortable and secure in a residential setting for a few days, why not take advantage of the opportunity? It seemed simple and straightforward.

Mother had his suitcase packed when I picked them up late in the morning. We would drop Dad off at the home and then I would take her to the airport. His room was clean and spare with a dresser for his underwear and extra clothing in a closet. After we had unpacked his clothes, we sat with him for awhile in the lobby where others were watching television. His speech was now garbled, but clear enough for us to understand as we hugged him in parting.

"So you're leaving me here?" he asked.

"Yes, Dad. Mother's going to Utah and she'll be back in four days."

"Oh," he turned his head away staring at the television screen. We hugged him again and left. As soon as we got to the car we both began to cry, the tears overflowing into sobs, but I started the engine and we drove away. Both of us realized that priorities had to be set. We could take care of ourselves or we could all travel to the cemetery with Dad in matching caskets. Mother was feeling the brunt of all the caretaking, but Dennis and I were wearing out, too. We needed some small window of relief.

Even so, my brother and his wife drove to Bellflower on Friday and Sunday, while Betty and I visited on Saturday and Monday. Dad seemed fine, but each time we left I cried and felt guilty. I knew the deep anguish that family members must feel when they place their parents in a nursing home permanently. This was only a four-day stay and my brother and I felt like the Menendez brothers. We had obviously lost perspective.

****

Dennis:

One of my most poignant memories was the visits that my wife Linda and I made to Brittany House in Bellflower. I'm sure that the set up and the drop off by Marilyn and Mom was painful and full of feelings, but I know what happened after they left.

Mehr

I went to the "home" in Bellflower shortly after Dad was, I believe against my mother's wishes, put there to give Mom a *break.* My father was *broken.* We talked, we traded, we laughed—he didn't belong there—I knew it—I didn't do anything about it—Damn! I sat with Dad for a long time in the patio area, we talked, then we returned through the glass doors with curtains (I can see them to this day) to his shared room. What a violation! This man would not undress alone in a dark room. Now strangers were going to bathe him and dress him because...

My wife Linda and I lowered Dad on to the bed, next to the night stand soon to be his head's best friend (he fell on it). We talked for about ten minutes and then the attendants arrived to announce, "Show time." This was the time to round up all of the unmanageables or violent clients along with the rest of them and put them in a circle to watch a movie. As we walked down the hallway to the circle a woman with, as I now appreciate, a problem or disease beyond my father's, began yelling at both of us. The people in charge took care of the person, at least temporarily, and wheeled her away. As Dad and I sat near the rear of the sleeping, nodding, drooling circle of movie goers, he said to me as he (observantly) scanned the circle, "THIS IS NO LIFE!" I looked my father in the eye and could say nothing. The movie that they had turned on was "On Golden Pond."

I said nothing. That night I held my father for one of the few times in my life. I loved him, I felt sorry for him, I felt *pissed off!* I went through the double "security" doors to my car crying harder with each step until I almost became convulsive. I sat in the car, opened the door and threw up until I felt as though my guts were being pulled through my throat. The thing that upset me most was the fact that *I* drove away from that place *alone.* My father was in there and as I look back on it, I *could* have changed it. I didn't and it's too *late, late, late...*

***

CHAPTER TEN

GOING HOME (1993-4)

Here, as the brain fails, the person becomes like a shadow,
like a reflection in a pool that is very, very blurry.
                              Jacob Fox, neurologist, *Time,* 1991

8/24/93 Nursing note: Wife stated that pt. had a fall on the curb. Wife's observation is that he is dizzy and more shaky since the fall. He wandered away from home last week and was found by paramedics, having fallen. Contused head then had another fall. Wife reports generally sleeping most of day. More confused in evening, "wants to go home." Refill meds.

T=94.8   P.=63   R.=18   B.P.=160/88   Wt.=178lbs.

M. Cardenas. RN

Marilyn:

I loved my work at the California School of Professional Psychology in Alhambra. CSPP was founded in the sixties by a group of radical therapists and professors who were frustrated with the academic training of psychologists. These idealistic reformers wanted to train clinicians who engaged with their communities and could talk to the people who lived in them. I liked the simmering mix of students and faculty endlessly stirring in the spice of different cultures and races. Here was the place where I could express my own contradictions as an unreconstructed liberal, a feminist and lesbian, as well as the daughter of Utah Mormon pioneers.

Even in the midst of all the debate and clamor, I still worried about my father. There was no way to escape the sense of impending doom, the feeling that I should be doing more. Every attempt at alleviating my mother's awesome burdens was thwarted. *Was she devoted to my father's care or was she just too damn cheap to spend the money?* I asked myself. My work gave me the structure I needed to keep from going berserk over my parents' worsening plight.

BROKEN CIRCUITS
A Memoir of Alzheimer's Disease in Four Voices

In the Fall of '93, I brought together fifty mental health workers from Los Angeles County for a retreat at Lake Arrowhead. The Simon Foundation had been generous in awarding me a grant to sponsor this workshop for "Women on the Front Lines," who needed a respite from the daily grind of poverty, helplessness and despair which they witnessed on their jobs. Of course, their response to my invitation was immediate and overwhelming. No one had ever noticed these women, nor their desperation. So, we met, talked, laughed, cried and wrote in our journals.

While I was intensely involved with these women, intent on making the weekend "work" for them, my thoughts still returned to Dad. He was leaving, departing in small gestures of frailty and confusion. There must be some way to hold him, I believed, to keep him from sliding further into the abyss of isolation and darkness. I knew he was going to die, but I wanted him to be aware, to know up until the last minute that he was loved. One afternoon, I asked the women at the retreat to write a dialogue with an important person. Mine was a make-believe conversation with Dad which began with a short description of his condition.

Mehr

My father is 82 years old and has Alzheimer's. He lives at home in with my Mother, his wife of 55 years. Once a big man whose presence filled the house, he is now slight and frail, hunched over and shuffling. He often stares vacantly into space, although he still seems to recognize me.

    M: Hi, Dad, how are you?

    D: Not so good, just good for nothing.

    M: Aw, Dad, c'mon. You're good for some things.

    D: For What?

(I think about his question for a few minutes and have no answer.)

    M: Well, I see what you mean. Not for yourself, anymore.

    D: Nope. 'Can't hear, can't taste, can't speak. No sex, no work, no church—what's left?

    M: We are, Dad. We need you. We need to know, all of us, that you're here. We still need to think of you, well, as a person.

BROKEN CIRCUITS
A Memoir of Alzheimer's Disease in Four Voices

D: But I'm not a person, not anymore. I'm just this old bag of bones, rattling about, eating, shitting, pissing in my pants. I'm not a person.

M: Yes, you are! You're still you!

D: It's not enough. I can't live this way anymore…I'm ready to go. There's nothing you need that I can give you.

M: (holding his hand and crying) We *can* get on without you, but we don't *want* to, Dad.

D: Well, I'll be 83 in March. That's enough. I've had a good life—better than my parents—I built a business, had a family, a marriage—not a good one, but I tried. Your mother did, too, so don't blame her for all the hurt. We did what we did.

M: I know. But the four of us can't accept that. We want you to love each other, really love each other, fiercely, and you won't or can't, I don't know what…so we keep hanging on and hoping…

D: We've made our peace. We won't get any closer. I wish we could have taught you more about

> love, but we didn't and it's too late. You'll just have to find your own way.
>
> M: I know, dammit.
>
> D: Find someone who's good enough for you, and give all you can—that's the key. (He laughs to himself) Yeah, but I couldn't do it, myself.
>
> M: I'm trying, Dad. And now, I've got to let you go. (He cries) It's all right. I'll be all right, don't cry.
>
> D: You sure?
>
> M: I'm sure.

The conversation between my father and me was an imaginary one, but it allowed me to give up on a lifelong project: helping my parents to love one another. Each of them carried into the marriage a heavy burden of deprivation and grief. Dad's parents had given up their friends, family and culture to arrive on the American frontier with few skills for survival. Lena tried to love her sons, but she was overwhelmed by her life. My maternal grandmother, Marcia, became the teenage mother of her own family. Both of my parents had grown up with orphaned parents who had learned the sober realities of work and poverty at an early age. As adults, they had little to give one another except their own unfulfilled needs. And so they fought, needling, ridiculing, jabbing and complaining, never able to ask for the love they truly wanted. This is their story. It will never have a happy ending.

As a therapist, I've tried to heal many families who have also experienced such deprivations. Sometimes, I've succeeded; other times, not at all. Whenever possible, I've obstinately tried to paste together the most fragmented of families because I know the price of bickering, accusation, withdrawal and heartbreak. With my own parents, the hurt and the bitterness of a half century of fighting would never be ameliorated, but each had often accepted his and her dependence on the other. I understood as I watched the sun set through the Ponderosa pines that now my father could live with the limited love he received. He had made his bargain and was at peace. At last, I could give up my role as a therapist to my own parents. My life was my own.

When my dear friend, Sam Matheny, became Chair of the Department of Family Practice at the University of Kentucky Medical School, he invited both Betty and me to join him on the faculty. We were both tempted by the opportunity to teach residents and medical students, so we visited Lexington in the Fall. It was a splendid time of year, all golden leaves and blue skies framing horse farms with big brick houses on the highest of hills. My father was continuing to decline, but my mother was coping, with the aid of Ruben, the homecare aide, who no longer ran away and was now the kind and watchful. He appeared just in time for breakfast and left at dusk. Still, I faced waves of guilt. How could I leave my parents at a time of their greatest need?

"Let's find out," Betty suggested. "We'll all get together and talk. You don't have to do this alone. I'll be there. We'll tell them what we want to do and then listen." It seemed so simple in the way she presented it that I called a family conference, this time without our old friend Dr. Ken. My Aunt Gladys and Uncle Hugh, as well as my mother's cousin Hazel, who were visiting my parents from Utah, were invited to join the after-dinner roundtable. Dennis showed up, knowing my plans, but still joking and covering his own anxiety over assuming an even greater responsibility for my parents. After we removed the last plates from the dinner table, we talked. I told everyone about this new opportunity in Kentucky, what it meant to me to become a professor in a medical school and how I could teach doctors to talk to patients. They all nodded and confirmed the need for doctors to have better training in relating to patients.

My voice became raspy as I tried to hold back tears, telling them how hard it would be to leave because I worried so much about Dad and Mom, how they would cope, what was coming next in their lives. My mother listened carefully, wanting to hold me fiercely, but realizing that she must finally let me go.

Finally, her sister said, "Well, Viv, what do you think? Can you manage without her?"

To her everlasting credit, my mother came through. She didn't laugh, didn't titter, didn't change the subject. She just said, "Yes, I think you should go." And she put her arms around me and held me close.

I talked to my brother who also reassured me that he could manage and that I should go. Then, I wrote to my two sisters, letting them know that after many years of looking after our parents, I was going to make a decision which would take me too far away to continue. The role of big sister in this family would now be shared. At fifty five years of age, I was free.

I met my brother at Baker's Square, our local meeting place. He slid into the booth across from me, smiling, but tense, his eyes showing the strain of holding a failing business together and holding himself together with too many years of hard living.

"What's up?" he asked, stirring his coffee.

"We're leaving, signed the contract."

"Good. I think you should." His hand shook only slightly as he stirred.

"What about you? Can you manage?"

"Sure. My business is headed south, my marriage has gone into receivership and my old man is dying. Don't worry.

We both started to laugh and then fell silent. I stirred my own coffee and he ordered a piece of pie.

"You don't mean it. You can't handle this."

"Yes, I can, just watch me."

He shrugged, then stood up, sat down beside me and put his arms around me just as Dad would have done.

"You're going and that's that, got it?"

"Got it."

He meant it. He had grown up, my kid brother. I could leave and he could take over. There were still three sisters who would back him up, but from a distance. It was time to tell my sisters.

Dear Nance and Judy, February 2, 1994

As you know, Betty and I have been deliberating for some time about accepting Sam's offer for jobs in Kentucky. At long last, we have decided to go and are heading East on June 15th. The offer is very sweet—economically and academically—and will allow us both to work with someone we know and value—our friend Sam, who is the Chair of the Family Practice Department. He has offered us a trial year to see how we get along with the natives and vice versa. We can both take leaves of absence from our schools so there is little risk other than the strain of moving from a house we have occupied and filled for twenty-some years. After the recent earthquake, however, the load is considerably lighter. You can't believe what our floors looked like when a crate of cranberry juice flew out of the closets on to a mound of kitchen crockery.

We both met with Mom, Aunt Glad, Uncle Hugh and Dad to discuss our plans. Mother says she can handle things with Ruben's help. There seems to be little relief for her and I worry about her own health. Is this the time to leave? At fifty five, I am finally leaving Los Angeles, just when my father has become totally lost and my mother drained dry. I am not an only child, though. We can all support her and share this awful guilt. She insists that I go and I believe her, but I pack with a heavy heart.

Love, Marilyn

So, I had announced my departure and everyone had given consent for me, the oldest child, the manager and chief, to leave. On July 1st, Betty and I loaded our brown and gold Jimmy with our Siberian husky Tasha for one last trip to Hollydale. Tasha was nearly 18 years old and had lived a remarkably long life for a husky. She would not survive a trip to Kentucky, and my mother had agreed to care for her until she died. We arranged a blanket in the garage, hugged her and gave her a milkbone, then cried, then walked the steps to the back door where we repeated the same leave-taking with my father.

He was, as Dr. Schneider's note recorded, "confused and unintelligible," but he squeezed my hand and smiled. He seemed to know that I was leaving although I wasn't sure. I knew and my mother knew. We hugged each other tightly, and then let go.

In the first few weeks following our arrival in Lexington, we spent most of our free time unpacking boxes and arranging furniture in our new apartment. In August, my sisters flew to California for Mother's seventy-eighth birthday where they were joined by our AFS sister, Gracie. As much as I wanted to be with them, I realized that I had to stay grounded in my new job. If this event were reason enough to leave, I would find a hundred more that were equally as persuasive. Instead, I waited for their reports.

****

Mehr

Judy:

Dear Marilyn,   August, 1994

'Glad I had a chance to talk with you and fill you in on Mother's birthday and Dad's condition. I was so depressed after our phone call. Jim says it is because "You haven't come to terms with your relationship with your parents." He's probably right, but I'm not sure how to do that. Sometimes I'm so angry with both of them for not really loving each other enough, then I'm sorry and guilty and I love them again. Pretty childish, huh? Then I'm mad at Mom for being a control freak and a health nut. And Dad for his horrible temper and inability to express a constant love for all of us. Besides, he's a hypocrite and I can't tolerate that in anyone.

Yet, both of them have always been there for us. I know they love me and my children and would do anything for us. What is that, except unconditional love? I think Mother is proud of me and I don't know if Dad is or not, but he was when he last knew what was going on. They love Jim, that's for sure. They made a home for us in which (even though somewhat weird at times) we had a fair amount of laughter, music, good books, ideas and in the end we've all grown up to be decent people.

I look at my kids and hope and pray that I can give them more than I received, but isn't that what Mom and Dad wanted for us—more than they received from their parents? I want to build a relationship with each of them that doesn't have the strain I feel with Mom and Dad, because I want to always feel the closeness, the honesty, the pure joy of being their mother and being in their presence. Oh well, thanks for listening.

Love, Judy

****

I went to Los Angeles to visit Mom and Dad, knowing that Gracie was also arriving from New York. We reminisced and enjoyed a few laughs, but we mostly worried about Mom and Dad—and Marilyn's dog, Tasha, who had been pronounced too "old" to travel with Marilyn to Kentucky. Gracie was very solicitous of the dog's welfare, so I let her do the "nursing" of the dog. But, I was the commandante that week for the family.

Mehr

Denny and I decided to have a birthday party for Mom and I asked Gracie to fix a favorite Argentinean dish, *Milanese*, which we would transport to Fullerton. She labored diligently, but the preparation took longer than we had expected and we arrived late.

Mom, Dad, Gracie and I soon pulled into the driveway and before long we were all enjoying some excellent dinner, the thin slices of lightly-breaded roast beef that Gracie had prepared for dinner. Dad now had his own wheelchair which Den rolled up to the end of the table. He was more adept at feeding himself this night, so we all relaxed and had fun teasing and joking with each other. Amongst our stupid remarks was a round of "Who's on first?" which we repeated *ad nauseum* until my sister-in-law threatened to throw us out if we didn't stop the game.

Anyway, it was soon time to leave. I drove home. As soon as we arrived, Mom was disgruntled and started fussing with Dad because he wasn't walking into the house fast enough. She burst out, "There's no reason why you just can't put one foot in front of the other!" He tried to balance himself among our helping hands, and remarked, "Oh, yes, there is."

She said, "Oh, yeah. What's that?" He retorted quickly, "My ass is out!" I looked down and saw that his Bermuda shorts were down about five inches from his waist baring his buttocks to the entire neighborhood! I grabbed his shorts and tried to pull them up without success. We all started laughing and he smiled, happy to win one more battle with his wife.

I remember this time because Dad was definitely losing control, shuffling, wetting his pants, wandering in the night. Mother was totally depleted, looking thin and nervous. If this caretaking lasted another year, Mother would be the one we would bury. I wanted to do something but Mother was stubborn about seeing this through on her own, so I let it pass, and went home.

****

Dennis:

What can I say about all of this? The more I think about my father's life, the more I realize that my own life mimics his, even though I try my damnedest to do it a little differently. Where did I learn to screw things up the way I have? The old man made mistakes, but they didn't come close to mine. The

Mehr

business has gone bust, my marriage is in the can and I haven't had a real conversation with my kids in ten years.

I try to imagine what it must have been like for Dad. He was used to being in control all the time, everywhere, and then he loses it. Near the end, he became so frustrated I was afraid he would really blow. It broke me up watching him—the glaze in the eyes, the stooped posture, the shuffling footsteps. All I could do was to offer support.

And now, the sonofabitch is taking off. There were things I wanted to ask him and now I never will. Nothing in this world makes me sadder right now than watching him shuffle up my driveway. There is no brew that has ever been made that can dull this pain, and believe me, I have tried to find one that will.

***

CHAPTER ELEVEN

A STILLNESS IN THE HOUSE

9/7/94 T=98.4   WT=wheelchair
       P=80   BP=120/70
       Age=83
       Subjective: Pt. has deteriorated significantly since last visit—increased falling, increased sleeping-Did not get lab work.
       Objective: lungs CTA, abdomen soft, non tender, ankle edema
       Assessment: Dementia/ALZ
                   Incontinent
       Plan: labwork CBC, PSA, SMA
       9/13/94 Pts. wife informed of PSA 11.5, TAF to Urology
                   (Signature) S. Kawasaki, DO/ Schneider, MD

Mehr

<u>Marilyn:</u>

Two days before my birthday, on October 6th, 1994, my brother called me, crying so hard he was unable to speak. At times, his sobs were so deep, I could only offer comfort.

"Hey, Den, it's all right. Whatever it is, tell me...we'll get through it."

"Dad's dying...Mother called hospice."

"All right, take care of each other...I'll be there tomorrow."

I flew home on the 7th to find the old German propped up on a hospital bed in the large airy den attached to the house. The room was light and smelled of the antiseptic that was used to treat his bedsores. He lay there on the white sheets dressed only in his undershirt, looking thin, white, emaciated and gasping for breath. I cried when I saw him. "Oh, Dad," I gasped, and reached out to kiss him as I held his head in my arms.

Throughout the night, Mother and I got up, fed him water through a syringe, rubbed his forehead and told him that we loved him. We also told him that he could let go whenever he wanted. We said that we could take care of ourselves and each other and would be all right. In the morning, when to the airport to pick up my sister Nancy, he was breathing in small, shallow flutters, no longer struggling to live.

When Nancy and I arrived from the airport at 9:15, she went directly to the sunroom that was now a hospital station. He lay there, his lips slightly parted as though caught in mid-sentence. She touched him and there was no response but the coldness of his bruised and emaciated arm. Quickly, she ran through the house to the front yard where she called to Ruben and me, "You'd better come, I think he's gone." As we hurried through the house, Mother joined us as we surrounded his bed in silence. The air seemed to have left the room, leaving only this great vacuum of stillness.

In an instant, Ruben pulled back the covers and began trying to resuscitate the body, pressing his palms feverishly against Dad's chest in short, regular bursts. There were a few sighs, soft cries the body makes when shocked against its will, but no willed response. Nancy and I locked eyes across the bed, sharing our secret hope that Ruben would not succeed. There was no need to prolong his suffering or ours. We wanted the struggle to be over, at last. And it was. After a few more intense pumps, the loyal manservant gave up. "I cannot do it," he apologized as he straightened Dad's pajamas and brought the sheet slowly to his neck. We nodded, offering easy forgiveness and deep gratitude for his limitations. One long decade of struggle was over.

Mother stood beside the bed studying Dad's face. "There's no need to call the mortuary," she told us, remembering her instructions from the hospice staff. The nurse said we should take our time." In a few moments, she and Nancy went into the kitchen, called Dennis and Judy and then returned to the stillness of our company. The four of us stood beside Dad's body watching as his arms and legs became whiter, his skin cooler, and his face set into a sly smile. At last, the wrackened breathing had stopped and the life seemed to be draining slowly from his body. He seemed to be at peace, his lips slightly parted as though marveling at some cosmic fanfare. We were as quiet as Quakers in a prayer meeting, contained in our own existential cocoons, contemplating the great silence of death.

After awhile, my mother found the list of steps to follow upon the death of a loved one, beginning with the reporting call. For all the years that I had walked the wards of hospitals with residents and physicians, I had never been present at the death of a patient. *What did one do?* I followed instructions, slowly dialing the number of the hospice. Someone answered immediately. I spoke softly, prepared to deliver a simple message. My father had died and the nurse should come to our home to sign the death certificate.

"My father..." I whispered and began to sob.

"Who?," the person asked.

"Alma...Alma Mehr."

"Can you spell her name, please?"

"Not *her, him*...Alma, *he* is a man."

"What relation is he to you?"

Again, the tears, surging like seizures through my body. "*Alma* is my father. He has just died." Then with unexpected pride, I added, "Yes, and he died in our home."

At last, she understood. "Someone will be over right away."

I returned to the room to tell the others the results of the hospice call. Then, my sister and mother went to the kitchen, while Ruben and I remained standing, keeping a silent vigil on either side of the body. Ruben touched him, folding his arms, straightening his legs as though preparing him for an afternoon nap. He still looked disheveled, his clothes matted with sweat. *There should be some dignity in death,* I thought. *At least he can dress up for his trip in the hearse.*

"Come on, Ruben, let's change his clothes."

He smiled, eager to fulfill his role once more. We pulled the frayed underwear over Dad's head, exposing the frail, eviscerated body. He looked like a tiny bird, his bony frame denuded of all but a few tufts of feathery hair, wisps of of silver creased at the sternum. We washed his upper body with soft towels, then Ruben removed the paper diaper fastened at the hips with Velcro and turned him on his side. I gasped at the raw red welts, the bedsores on his hips and knees where the bone had broken through his skin from sustained pressure. The wounds were dark crimson at the center, ringed with pink flesh, then haloed by a white antiseptic powder. He was a war map of oozing raw craters. I drew back, stunned, angry and guilty. *How could this have happened?*

Unaware of my anguish, Ruben once again turned him over on his back, exposing his stomach and groin, still tufted with soft white hairs like a youth's. Deftly, Ruben removed the bandages holding a catheter in place, then wrapped everything, gauze and tubing into a neat package. Then, he wiped him softly with a tissue and slipped the undershorts over Dad's legs. Together we clothed him in clean flannel pajamas, neatly buttoned at the neck as he always wore them. *May you feel loved in your dying,* I implored, wanting the worn cotton to soothe and give him comfort. Still, he looked so vulnerable. I wanted strangers to see him as a kindly, old man in a new pair of pajamas, clean and composed, prepared for their ministrations.

"Ruben, let's get his bathrobe." He smiled and slipped away to find the covering that would give his body dignity. Immediately, he returned with a royal blue robe with bright crimson piping around the sleeves and collar.

"Perfect, Ruben, perfect."

We worked together as I held Dad, helping to slip his arms into the opening of the robe as Ruben brought the cloth over his midsection and tied the belt neatly at his waist. Then we lowered him down onto the bed, propped his head against a clean white pillow and folded his arms neatly across his chest. Mr. Alma Mehr was ready to meet his guests.

The first to arrive was a Filipino nurse from hospice. She embraced each of us, expressing sympathy, then asked for the time of death. I said 9:00, my sister and mother nodded and the nurse seemed satisfied. Her name was Marta and she seemed to be completely at home in the presence of a corpse.

Marta spoke to Ruben in Spanish, then left, hugging us all once more. My brother passed her in the driveway, then shortly appeared at the back door of the kitchen. We each hugged him and cried some more. He walked slowly down the steps into the room where my father lay. The son bent over the bed and stroked his father's head, smoothing back the tendrils of white hair that curled at his temple, letting his tears bathe Dad's face.

My mother watched, unable to sustain the silence and asked, "What about a mortuary? Who should we call?"

"Mom," I whispered, "Let's talk about it in the living room." It was hard to mask the frustration I felt. My brother needed time and she needed a plan. The three women departed for the parlor, Ruben went outside to water the lawn, and my brother stayed behind to say his farewells in private.

When it came to the knowledge of mortuaries—how they work, where they are, who does what—my mother was an expert. Since we were children, she had played the organ for funeral services in mortuaries throughout nearby communities. She knew the funeral directors by name, the make and model of their musical equipment, the styles of their services.

"We could call Downey Mortuary," she considered. "It used to be owned by Dave Chandler, you remember him, don't you both?" We nodded in unison, complicit in a shared memory of a Christmas long ago when Dad chased Nancy outside the house while Dave and his new wife escaped to the safety of their big blue Buick. "Well, Dave died long ago and I think it's owned by an Armenian fellow. I can't think of his name."

She then reviewed several other names and decided upon one owned by a Bishop of the Mormon church, Allen-English and Estrada, the logo for the new Bell Gardens. It was amazing how quickly we reached consensus, making just the right decisions. *So this is how a family works,* I thought, *when there is no one around to stir up discord. Had it not been for him, we might have lived in harmony.* I couldn't allow myself to entertain this thought for very long, so I called the mortuary to ask for a hearse.

A knock on the door announced the presence of Mother's own bishop, Boyd Benson. He was dressed formally, in a slick gray suit, a blue-eyed Irishman with rheumy eyes who expressed condolences and slid through the house into the den to perform his duties as representative of the church. My mother pursued him, determined to hold him accountable for the neglect she had felt during these hard and lonely years.

"Well, Bishop, where have *you* been?"

Startled, he stepped back to encounter my mother's anger. "I've been here, Sister Mehr."

"No, you haven't. You haven't set foot in this house in six months!"

"Yes, I have. I was here last week!"

"You were not! You were never here when we needed you!"

I loved my mother's anger, sharp, challenging and unrelenting. She had contained her fury for years and was now ready to unleash it, not at the church itself, but upon one of its failed emissaries. She could be angry at Boyd Benson, a bishop who had proved to be an imperfect vessel, but one that, nonetheless, needed scolding. The church was, well, the church, perfect and inviolate.

Leaving them to their battle, I went back to the living room and stood looking through the front window where Dad's red truck was always parked. I could almost hear the echoes of the voices of children playing on the front lawn, calling "Red Rover, Red Rover, I dare you to come over!" as the truck pulled in at dusk and everyone broke up the game, running to greet this dark and burly man, jump into his arms, feel the warmth of his great body, the rough edge of his jacket and the safety of his wide embrace.

My reverie was interrupted by a company of family and clergy. Boyd and mother had made peace with each other and were ready to form a prayer circle. I reached out my right hand to my sister, my left to my brother, while they offered an extra hand to my mother. Whether we all believed in God or not, we wanted to form a circle, to hold each other's arms like links in a chain, now absent my father. Boyd mumbled a prayer asking

Mehr

that death bring compassion and forgiveness, probably as much for himself as for Dad, and then left promptly before Mother decided to settle other insults. Judy arrived on Sunday and we three sisters spent a quiet weekend together before the nieces and nephews began arriving, remembering Dad, good times and bad.

I called Betty after the Bishop left, to tell her that Dad had died. She was sympathetic, at first, then sharply added, "You don't expect me to come to the funeral, do you?"

"Well, yes, I do, of course, I do. Isn't this what family is? Showing up when people die?"

She was adamant. "I'm not coming and I can't believe you would ask me. You know what I think of the way your mother treated your father."

"And how will your absence drive home that point?" I asked. I want you to come here for *me*!"

The argument went on, but our positions never changed. I was deeply hurt and saw her response as a clear sign that she really didn't love me, not enough to overcome her anger and show up. She believed that there was no place for her in my family's ceremonies, still returning to her marginal place at the golden anniversary party. I knew what she meant, how ceremonies and rituals force a family to make public declarations, but I reassured her that this time, I wouldn't waiver, that she would be at my side.

"I'm sorry," she finally said, "but I'm not coming."

I hung up the phone and called my friend, Sam, to share my own disappointment and hurt. It would have been easy for him to side with me because he's always felt closer to me than Betty. To his credit, he listened, sighed heavily, then counseled.

"Marilyn, she was there for you before he died and she will be there for you afterwards. She's just not coming to your father's funeral."

At the time, it wasn't enough to console me, and I reached out to the extended family I have made for myself, a family of dear friends who have shared weddings, births, divorces and deaths. There are six of them, all women, all accomplished and talented women would answer a call from me from any spot on the globe, any time of the night or day. This time, I dialed the numbers of two fellow therapists, Diana Taylor and Bea Daccardi. I told each of them about my father's death, Betty's refusal to appear. Bea listened and said, "We'll be there, no question...and she'll hear from us, Italian style!" They drove from their Bel-Air enclaves across the wide expanse of L.A. to this plain stucco church in the suburbs, sat through a two-hour Mormon funeral, looking fully gorgeous, my two beautiful adopted sisters, warm, Latin, big-hearted. How I loved them on that day!

Their presence didn't repair the tear in Betty's and my relationship, but it enabled me to feel support from outside of my family, to feel a connection with the people who knew me as I was now. The funeral was held in the local ward chapel filled with friends and family whose lives had been touched by Dad: missionaries who had received monthly stipends, elders from the church, kids from Bell Gardens high school who had received scholarships, and his brother Nephi, whose eerie resemblance to Dad brought tears to our eyes. Cousins and friends arrived from everywhere as well as many long time friends.

Mormon funerals are usually a combination of biography and scripture, punctuated by pioneer hymns and lengthy prayers. Someone usually tells the life story, then others preach a sermon. I wanted to tell the story. I wanted the audience to know about my father: his poor beginnings, his optimism and energy in starting a business, his generosity to his family and others, and yes, his temper and his meanness. This was but a man, I wanted them to know, who needed no larger imprint than the one he made. But, be clear. He did leave his mark.

I worried that I would not be able to tell the story without weeping. Finally, I decided to stuff my pockets full of tissues and allow the tears to roll. They did and I continued to talk. I wanted to tell his story. Afterwards, my brothers-in-law, Lee Snell and Jim Olson, mixed scripture with their own memories. And then, the children sang, all of them, all thirteen of the grandchildren, a medley of songs Dad had loved. I was fairly composed until they began to sing "The Red River Valley." I wept until my body shook. My Aunt Gladys held me in her arms as though sheltering an eight-year old. What is it about a group of kids singing a cowboy song off-key that finally touches the heart? It was tender, loving, beautiful.

Then, our AFS sister, Graciela, stood on two hymn books to boost herself to the edge of the podium and talked about her "American Dad."

Mehr

"Many years ago, in 1962, I was a foreign exchange student in California and lived with a wonderful family—The Mehr's. It was an experience that would mark me for the rest of my life. After I returned home, we wrote to each other for several years and Mr. Mehr, my Dad, even came to Argentina to visit me and my family. Unfortunately, as the years went by, we stopped writing and we lost track of each other.

That is, until 1992, when I was sent to New York by the U.N. for a special on-the-job training program. I began to think about calling the Mehr's, a family that had been present in my thoughts and heart for so many years. I didn't know whether I could find the courage to call them: *Have they moved? Would they remember me?* Finally, I called.

It was late on a Friday evening, July 9th or 10th. I was alone in the office and decided to dial the phone. As it continued to ring, I felt that my heart was going to burst.

"Hello!" I recognized my Mother's voice.

"Is this the Mehr family?"

"Yes, it is."

"Is this Mrs. Mehr?"

"Yes…"

"Mom, this is Gracie."

"Gracie, is this you? I can't believe it!"

At that moment, I knew that we had been very close to each other for all those years, despite the distance, despite the silence. I talked to Mom, and then to Dad. My feelings of love and joy were overwhelming. I had recovered something that was very important in my life that I believed was gone forever. All of a sudden it came back to me.

"Gracie, you have made my day!" were Mom's parting words.

I went back to my apartment feeling like the happiest woman on earth. As I opened the door, the telephone rang. My sister Judy, calling from Texas! Then, it rang again and this time it was Marilyn, calling from New York. She had just come back from a vacation in Europe and was staying in the city. In less than half an hour she jumped on the First Avenue bus and met me in front of the U.N. We talked into the morning hours, then agreed to meet just as soon as all of the Mehr's could get together in Los Angeles.

Within a month, I was flying west. As I got out of the car, Mrs. Mehr came rushing out of the front door, followed by

Mehr

Marilyn, Nancy, Judy and Denny who brought Dad into our circle of weeping women. He, too, wept and so did my adopted brother. I'm so glad I had time for our reunion and I dedicate this poem to my American father:

> En Paz
> by Amado Nervo

> Muy cerca de mi ocaso, yo te bendigo, Vida,
> porque nunca me diste ni esperanza fallida,
> ni trabajos injustos, ni pena inmerecida;

> porque veo, al final de mi rudo camino,
> que yo fui el arquitecto de mi propio destino;

> que si extraje las mieles o la hiel de las cosas,
> fue poeque en ella puse hiel o mieles sabrosas:
> cuando plante' rosales coseche siempre rosas.

> …Cierto, a mis lozani'as va a seguir el invierno:
> !mas tu no me dijiste que mayo fuese eterno!

> Halle' sin duda largas las noches de mis penas;
> mas no me prometiste tu so'lo noches buenas;
> y en cambio, tuve algunas santamente serenas…

> Ame', fui amado, el sol acaricio mi faz.
> !Vida, nada me debes! Vida, estamos en paz!

BROKEN CIRCUITS
A Memoir of Alzheimer's Disease in Four Voices

Many in the audience did not understand Spanish, but they understood the deep feeling in her voice and saw the tears streaming down her cheeks. For them, she read a translation:

In Peace
by Amado Nervo

Close to my end, I bless you, Life,
because you never gave me false hope,
nor unfair labor, nor undeserved pain;

because I see, at the end of my rough road,
that I have been the architect of my own destiny;

that if I extracted honey or bile from life,
it was because I had given bile or delicious honey;
when I sowed roses I always reaped roses.

…It is true, my health will be followed by winter;
but you never told me that May would be eternal!

I certainly found long the nights of my sorrows;
But you never promised me only good nights;
and, conversely, I had blessed and serene ones…

I loved, I was loved, the sun caressed my face.
Life, you don't owe me anything! Life, we are at peace!

Mehr

After the funeral, we all drove to the Rose Hills cemetery, where the casket lay on a green hillside festooned with flowers. Mother seemed to be sleepwalking through most of the day, her body, floating from person to person, opaquely and without real substance. At last, she stood wanly at the front doorstep, waving to each group of family members who drove away.

Mother was now truly alone. In the following weeks, I worried that she might find the silence unbearable, but each time I called, she reassured me that she was all right. "Don't worry," she admonished me, to no avail. I still worried. On subsequent phone calls, she seemed so vague and disconnected. "When did your Dad die? Who was there? Did Jim speak, the bishop? Does my sister Gladys know?" I answered each question carefully, but nothing seemed to find a home in her brain. Finally, I wrote to her, hoping to piece together some of the events of the week surrounding Dad's death.

BROKEN CIRCUITS
A Memoir of Alzheimer's Disease in Four Voices

Dear Mom,   October 14, 1996

I'm so glad we had the chance to be together in the week after Dad's death. Because there were so many conversations, I thought it might be helpful to summarize some of the ideas we agreed upon so that later you can think, act, change your mind, talk to other family members, whatever.

First, you asked several times about the chronology of the week preceding Dad's death. As I understand it, the Elders assembled on Wednesday night and gave Dad a blessing in which they gave him permission to release himself from this life and his obligations. Claudel Empey, his fellow elder, assured him that we would get along all right, that he no longer needed to feel responsible for us. I guess it is now up to us to show that we can get along, even though we all miss Dad so much.

Anyway, on Thursday, Denny came over to help with Dad and was so overcome by his condition that he called Nance and asked her to call me and Judy, which she did. I arrived on Friday and spent the day and evening with you and Dad. We both tried to make him feel comfortable by keeping fluids in him, but he was not responsive. His breathing was labored and he struggled so hard just to continue living. He finally gave up, minutes before I came back from the airport where I had picked Nancy up, Saturday morning.

After he died, you and Nancy began to call family members, while Reuben and I changed his clothes and prepared him for his trip to the mortuary. Denny arrived soon after and we sat with him for awhile in silence. Then, the nurse from hospice arrived. She was wonderful, hugging everyone and reassuring us that his death was a blessing. I don't know whether it was, but at least it's a relief. Shortly, Boyd Benson appeared and we all formed a prayer circle. After that, your neighbor, CiCi arrived with her little boy Daniel, overflowing with large Latin tears and she, too, hugged and kissed everyone, including Dad. It was a peaceful and loving passing.

You have asked me about my intentions to stay in Kentucky. I'm really enjoying the work here, feel well compensated and appreciated. Sam would like me to stay for an additional year while I continue to set up the Behavioral Science department. I do not want to stay here forever, but I have enjoyed the people and the University setting enough to continue for another year. I know you'll miss me, but as

Gracie's mother put it, "Your children will go on with their lives and so will you."

All of which brings us to the future. You've spoken many times about the difficulty of moving. If you should ever decide to move, say to Leisure World or Sun City, we would all pitch in to help you sort, pack, unpack and settle in to your new home. If you decide to stay put, that's fine, too. However, we talked about how easy it is to become isolated in Hollydale how necessary it is to reach out to others through going to classes or taking trips. We also talked about how many resources you have to offer to others, perhaps as a teacher's aide at an elementary school to assist in reading programs. You have a good education and a fine mind which could enable others to enjoy some of the things that have meant so much to you.

Please know that we all love you and want the best for you. I realize that it will take time to recover from a decade of caregiving and that you'll proceed at your own pace. Let's keep talking, all of us, so that the life you now have is one in which you feel loved and challenged.

Love, Marilyn

Mehr

The four of us had always been connected to each other like spokes of a wheel fastened to the hub of our parents. We had rarely visited each other just to meet as sisters and brother, but had come together for celebrations for our parents. Now, we began to explore, tentatively, at first, our relationships with one another. How much did we care about one another as friends. Had our past experiences as children touched us deeply enough to make us want to tie these threads into adulthood, without the need of any longer caring for an ailing father? We would see.

****

Judy:

Huntsville, Texas

Dear Marilyn, Nancy and Den, October 18, 1994

Yesterday, in a symbolic sort of way, I finished my nervous knitting and put my afghan away. Maybe finishing it means I'm ready to return to normal. Yet, there are all kinds of reflections in my head. First and most, I am so glad we were able to share together our feelings of loss and celebration — first, with the four of us alone, and then, with the others. I knew right away that I needed Jim, but didn't realize what a comfort it would be to have my children with me.

The service was just what Mom wanted and needed and, I think, what Dad would have wanted. There's no denying that he believed strongly in the resurrection of the dead and that hope sustains me. When I die, I want lots of music and flowers, just like Dad. Den was right about choosing the mahogany casket and the autumn flower arrangement—all perfect. I loved the congregational music and the songs the kids sang, "It's A Long, Long Trail A-Winding," and then, "The Red River Valley." So very beautiful.

Using the old red Ford as a hearse was wonderful. For awhile, I'm carrying the photos in my wallet, just to hold on to the memory of Den driving slowly past the store carrying Dad's casket in the bed of the truck.

It was so hard for me to see him lying there so still and so dead. I've pondered about Dad's legacy for us. He showed us how to work hard and long, how to laugh at fools, how to love one another. He taught us that a good man can also be an angry man and a mean one.

Mehr

Thanks to all of you. I love you and treasure the memories we share. We have now gotten together in five year intervals since 1985. Any interest in trying again this summer? I'm sure Mother would love it. Would we? Let me know, but don't think about it too, long. Call me.

Much love, Judy

****

<u>Dennis:</u>

The funeral was an extremely hard time for me. After being locked at the hip with my old man for twenty-five years, I was free, but I realize that the hard, nasty German had quite an impact on my life. All those years we spent together at the shop were not all bad. He just never seemed to be happy.

His kids never had the challenges that he had so it's hard for me to pass judgment on him. He did what he thought he had to do and did it the only way he knew how. It wasn't my job to like it. I wish we could have had a good relationship, but we didn't. He never had a good one with Mother. Yet, he did a lot for people. There are plenty of people in Bell Gardens who will tell you that he was the greatest man ever born.

BROKEN CIRCUITS
A Memoir of Alzheimer's Disease in Four Voices

He had one friend, John Christoff, a real friend. John still comes by the shop, cooks up a pot of chili and tells stories about Dad. They both came from tough backgrounds. Maybe that's what they understood about each other.

He was never a soldier, but someone who had been out of my life for some thirty years heard of my father's death sent me a flag that had been flown over the capital in his name. She had listened to me and after trying to talk to me, called her senator in Florida who had sent the flag. I think to this day, and quite probably, until the day that I die, that this is the most special gift that I have *ever* received.

I don't believe that we are forced to look at our mortality, but I am grateful that I have been permitted (for whatever reason) to step back and *see.* It's amazing to me now how easy that it can be to, in this short stay, lose all sight of the <u>real</u>. I actually don't think it takes that much to see it all clearly, but I haven't wanted to. Now, I can and I'm going to make some tough choices. For the first time, people are going to see the real person that I am. That's okay because it will be the real me.

***

CHAPTER TWELVE

MOURNING AND REMEMBERING

Christmas 1994

Dear Judy, Jim, Den, Linda, Nance, Lee, Mom, Gracie and Marcelo,

It's true, the best time of the year can also be the worst. Memories, just when you least expect them, jump up on your back when you're just strolling around Macy's and bite your neck, leaving you stunned and disoriented, kind of weak and panicked. But, I won't wait for them to attack me, I'll go looking for them myself, seek out the dark corners where they lurk and shine a light right in their faces. That's hard, too, you bet, but least you can feel a tiny sense of control.

Mehr

Memories...I was talking to Den yesterday about our trips to Logan as kids and all he had to say was "Bakersfield," and in that shorthand that is family-talk, we both knew what he meant. Neither of us had to describe the car and the trailer beside the highway, wobbling to and fro as Mom and Dad fought, and the trucks whipped us like skeet. Phyllis Diller once said, "Never go to bed angry, stay up and fight!" and I knew our parents would agree.

The memories I have at this time are often sad. I remember Dad's generosity at Christmas and his pleasure in giving to us when we were small, but I also remember how the season evoked his own feelings of deprivation which he frequently expressed in outbursts of anger and rage. That's not in the calendar and I don't want it to be. I hope that what comes through is what I meant: snapshots of a life, the yearnings of a young man, then a couple gazing at the future, then kids and friends, an anniversary and some travels and finally, one last slow run in a red pickup truck.

I suppose the take-home message is to live each day fully, to turn the light on the demons in the corners, and to take at least one vitamin C every day. I hope that you are well and know that I'll be thinking of you during the season. Betty and I will be in New York, enjoying the city, seeing Gracie and Marcelo, and visiting Betty's Mother and Alex who have just acquired two spaniel pups. There's a vote for the future!

And don't forget. Come and visit the Bluegrass!

Love, Marilyn

****

Judy:

When I returned home to Texas after the funeral, I began to think of Dad being somewhere peaceful, as his purest self. I could see him talking with his great grandchildren, Synneve, London, and Benjamin, telling the story of his life. He'd kiss them, each one, and send them on their way.

The four of Dad's kids managed to reconcile, too. My brother "allowed" me to hug him at the funeral home, albeit stiffly. Anyway, he called me at Christmas, thanks to my son, and it was nice for me and for Brad. A few times, after the funeral week, I would call Brad, "Den," because he reminded me of my brother when he was just becoming a teenager, the last time we were ever close.

Mehr

During this past month, I've suffered a pretty serious depression that I couldn't crawl away from. I've cried a lot and kept to myself. The word I kept saying was "extraneous." The doctor prescribed Zoloft and it seemed to help.

I never really told Dad about my feelings for him and I regret that. Now, I have a chance to make it right with my own kids. "Learning from the past," that's the best I can do. This is Brad's senior year and I've cried a lot about his leaving. He's such a special kid, so talented and smart, but just so natural and loving. Heather and Karin are both pregnant, so we'll have two more granddaughters. This must be the season of my grandmothering. I like it a lot. Sometimes it's hard for me to remember the good things. It's not like they never happened, but I have a hard time remembering anything good. So, I've tried to remember something happy:

- Christmas music. Thanks to Mom, I've always loved to sing. Remember Thora and Priscilla singing *Silver Bells?* And Sister Guinn singing tenor while her goofy little boy patted mom's breasts? And the *Littlest Angel* with Loretta Young narrating?

- Trips to L.A. to see the Christmas windows. Every holiday season, we all crammed into the Ford and drove downtown to see the wonderful animated displays in the store windows. Dad would always caution us just as we crossed over the railroad tracks at Alameda, "O.K., kids, roll up those windows and lock the doors. We're going *uptown* now!"

- Playing Santa. Dad wanted to make sure that no one in the church was needy so he always loaded up a little red wagon and delivered a stack of groceries and toys to a neighbor a few blocks away. The greedy little kids wanted the wagon, too. Dad bought the kid off with a box of See's candies, but he wasn't entirely satisfied.

This year I'm fifty-one and Jim is fifty. I feel as though we're at a midpoint when it's time to forget my own childhood and concentrate on the future...my grandchildren. They give me hope.

****

<u>Nancy:</u>

I've been thinking a lot about my Dad since he died, trying to sum up who he was and what he meant to me. I know that he was a hard worker and charitable—generous to a fault. As the second daughter, I still don't understand his sudden outbursts of anger, how he could be so emotionally fickle that you didn't know where to run or hide. When things got hot, I usually caught the brunt of his anger. Mostly, I stayed and fought, not always head-on collisions, more often wisecracks and verbal cartoons, but I didn't let him bully me. The old man was not going to win!

I remember one night when I had just started driving, just sixteen years old, I asked him for the credit card. As a typical teenager who assumed she had a right to her parents' money, I thought the request was no big deal. I was "wrong," of course. My Dad was feeling unappreciated (I suppose), so he attacked, "Take, take, take. That's all you kids ever do!" I never forgot the look of malice on his face or the anger in his voice.

My father had this free-flowing generosity laced with a horrible tendency to feel unappreciated. Still, he contributed heavily to the church all his life, 10% of his income to tithing, more money for the Ward Building Fund, stipends for missionaries, special collections for needy families, and so on. In his last years, Dad would sometimes forget and accidentally pay his tithing twice. I'm sure he really didn't care, but the Ward Clerk would refund the check to Mother, which she gratefully accepted. Dad had always willingly paid more than his "fair share" and he wanted his children to have more than he had.

One windy night "on Highland," as Dad called our little town, he couldn't sleep—worrying how Lee and I could feed and provide for our seven children. Mom told me about it the next morning. I was very touched, especially since he had been so angry at both Lee and me through the years when we ran short of money and asked him for loans. Anyhow, it wasn't long before the Mehr Family Educational Trust was established. For ten years our children paid tuition, bought books and clothes and traveled on the money bequeathed by the trust. I realize that Mom allowed Dad to be the "hero" in setting up the trust, although she probably did most of the work and ironed out the legal details. I remember his generosity to me and my children and try to believe that he did loved me as a child, but that love was camouflaged with too much anger.

When you sum it all up, our lives together, I wonder how I can say, "Thanks, Dad, for all you did for us?" I used to rationalize that I could do it by living a good life, but I was wrong. That's not enough. The last few years I tried to do more than that, visiting my parents for as many days as I could "tolerate." I wanted to make up for all those years of my narrow judging, my inability to understand his life and its hardships. I hope in my own way that I eased the struggles of their last years together.

I always sympathized with my mother and resented anyone who criticized her. After all, she lived with my father, the bonehead. She endured over fifty-five years with him, waiting for the reward of a happy old-age together. Then, she's faced with the trials of almost ten years with a husband in a long slow slide into Alzheimer's disease. Stubborn as the Irish, she refused to put him in a "rest" home, insisting that he live and die in his home. There were many who criticized her for it, but she did what she believed was best.

I was glad I was there when he died. 'Just moments after I arrived from the airport, I went to the kitchen to put some raspberry jam in the freezer, then went to the sunporch where he lay on a hospital bed. My sister had told me how bad he was while we were driving along the Century Freeway, but I couldn't believe he would die, not yet. His fierce peasant heart was just too strong to give up. I stepped into the room and saw him there, still, pale and without any movement—no heart beat, no breathing, no life.

The priesthood brethren had given him a blessing, releasing him from this life, but he had struggled on until we drove into the driveway, until we could surround him and still feel the warmth of his body in those quiet moments after his death. We'll miss you, Dad. But we've missed you for quite awhile already.

****

Mehr

<u>Dennis:</u>

As his only son, I think about Dad with a mixed bag of feelings—some fear, some respect. There are questions that will never be answered, such as why he carried this shotgun inside of himself that could go off without notice; such as why he and I never had a real talk; such as, why he didn't see the trouble I was in as a teenager and try to stop me; such as why neither of us ever told the other that we loved each other.

He had some observations on life that, as time goes by, I have begun to respect. He was a good judge of character. He was smart. He was mean, but he did it with a purpose.

I thought I was okay after he died. I've been around death in business here and there, but other than losing older grandparents, I don't think I even knew what a tough Son of a Bitch it could be.

I still, now, have to stop because I break down and can't explain why. Nothing seems to be going right in my life and losing my old man is just one more damn failure.

I'm not the only one to lose a parent on this planet. Does everyone feel this way? Maybe watching him as he was eaten by this monster, being taken a day at a time, piece at a time—

his self-esteem, his strength, his physical being has just eaten me up, too. It wasn't fair and I know, yes, that life is unfair, but goddammit, it wasn't right.

I miss the nasty S.O.B.

****

<u>Marilyn:</u>

Christmas 1994

Betty and I are in New York...once more...for a Christmas holiday. It's the 26th of December, and I'm mixing with the tourists along Fifth Avenue, bumping and sliding like so many minnows swimming in a slush-filled pond. I pause for a brief visit to a Barnes and Noble, push through the revolving doors and maneuver along the outside walls to the Women's Fiction section to make a quick scan of the new gender books. Deborah Tannen on power and dominance, how language let's us hammer other people, too often women, into mute submission; Gloria Steinem, singing a chorus or two on self-esteem and mid-life contentment. Let's see what we have here...aha! a chapter on, "Turning 60," by Carolyn Heilbrun, who wants us to know that it's not just a piece of cake!

However, she does seem convinced that a woman at 69 can finally find the source of power from within so that others can be damned and you can find your own way. Then, on to the recitative Gail Sheehy, begging forgiveness for saying that life was over at forty, and yes, it does go on and on and on, and ever so much better. I can hardly wait to be 100!

My head is spinning as I whirl through the doorway and back on to the street with the spires of St. Patrick's looming in my face. All right, I'll enter, get spiritual, see what happens. The vast inner chamber is festooned with red poinsettia, the color of Christ's blood, right? Everywhere, poinsettia. A small Irish priest in a white robe intones a mass as hundreds of onlookers chatter along the corridors. Is everyone so oblivious that they genuflect at the patriarchal altar or is denial the gift of the season? It's time to head for Saks.

Age be damned, to hell with religion, find salvation in Saks. Even more worshippers, here, all huddled before the altars of cosmetic companies, slender kohl-eyed clerks spraying mists of cologne on the heads of supplicants. I bump and push along with the scented hordes until I reach the escalator and let myself be lifted over and over again until I see "Seventh Floor:

Coats." There they are in rows and racks, coats, coats, coats, hundreds and hundreds of them, camel, blue, black, wool, leather, polyester, long, medium, short, everywhere I turn I can see coats. I feel wrapped up, stuffed and suffocated. It's too much, there are too many, abundance and excess, and I flee once more to the crowded street below. A few blocks more, then right on Fifth, over to Sixth, then Seventh, to the ticket window of "The Inspector Calls," where I buy two tickets for Betty and me in the Mezzanine. Perhaps, later, we shall both find enlightenment.

Proud of myself, I retrace my steps along 45th, past Times Square, over on Park, down the steps of Grand Central. I can still hear the voices of the radio announcer as the sounds of the massive engines draw nearer to the station, "City of a million dreams, crossroads of the world," as I enter the expanse of this great cavern. Splashes of red everywhere, just like St. Pat's. Only this time it's probably the blood of the homeless oozing up from the subway caverns below.

Hardly breathing, I am out in the street again, left on Third Avenue where a sweet young girl from Yellow Springs, Ohio, asks me directions to Sam Goody's. I think I know, or do

I? She's not sure she can believe my answer. "How about Tower Records?" I offer. I *know* where that is. She suspects otherwise and turns to a Pakistani street vendor who points and gestures and seems definite in his knowledge of the city.

She knows where she's going and so do I—Citicorp Building on 53rd. My legs are starting to ache from my wanderings so I hurry my pace, hoping for a chair in the Atrium where I can have a coffee and rest. Not to be. The seats are filled with an audience of acolytes of Jewish music, a band, four men in dark suits and yarmulkes, pounding out the beat of "Havalaya," an ode to the New Year. The music surges, the audience claps and three old Jews get to their feet, a woman with white hair, a slightly stooped old man, an old gnome from the Romanian Forests, hair flying, a great long beard and a knapsack. He begins twirling like a gnarled dervish, then he spins the man and the woman in circles, faster and smaller. He dances with both of them at once and they are entranced, raising their hands, palms skyward in hopes for the New Year. It is a moment of wonder.

And it is over in a flash as people applaud, bundle themselves in their coats and scarves and ascend the steps at

BROKEN CIRCUITS
A Memoir of Alzheimer's Disease in Four Voices

the four points of the compass and depart. Now, I can find a chair anywhere, so I buy a turkey sandwich and a cream soda and remember other seasons. For some reason, I think of a Christmas, in 1956, and recall an image of Dad chasing my younger sister Nancy around the Christmas tree with a drumstick in his hand, Mother is crying, holding the babies, Judy and Denny, and I'm hiding in the corner. I awaken from this reverie with a jolt, overcome with tears and sorrow.

Where is Conran's? I wonder. Like my past, Conran's no longer exists and has, in fact, become Barnes and Noble. I climb the steps to the entrance of the store and wander among the stacks stopping at the psychology section. This time I pull a book off the shelf by a fellow Californian, a Jungian therapist from UCLA, writing about how daughters and fathers must separate and what happens when they don't. With the death of my own father just two months past, I am fascinated as I prop myself against the bookcase reading, scanning, trying to swallow the paragraphs in large gulps. The author believes that fathers choose a favorite daughter, make her a confidante and disparage the mother, who is seen as weak and pitiful. Naturally, the daughter identifies with the father, takes on his traits, learns to hold her feelings in, wants to please him, becomes ambitious and denies her "feminine" side, then loses touch with her creativity and capacity for intimacy. It is often only when he dies that she returns to her own injuries, seeking to heal and redress them. *Yes,* I say to myself, *I know this woman!*

I put the book under my arm and stagger to the Starbuck's counter for a large infusion of caffeine. Leaning upon the bar stool, I prepare myself for a small epiphany. This is it, then, the moment of redemption, in which we, the women of this generation, move from waving the banner of power and dominance, surge through the mantras of self-esteem and sixties, make those passages, open those doors and there's Dad. *Step aside, Papa,* I want to say, *your daughter is on her way, dancing in a red sea of poinsettia, finding the song that is her own.* The words from one of Dylan's old 60's tunes resonate in my ears, "Freedom's just another word for nothing left to lose," and in this sweet moment of transcendence, I know it is true.

***

EPILOGUE

A NEW FAMILY-1996

<u>Nancy:</u>

I had mixed feelings about organizing a birthday party for Mom, but Marilyn thought it was a good idea and Mother was going to be eighty years old, after all. My sister has these good ideas, especially when she lives two-thousand miles away and I live right next to the birthday park. I'm still not hot on initiating large work projects, ever since Dad died. I just don't have the enthusiasm for family gatherings. Besides, our second daughter, Carrie, was leaving for a mission for the church and I needed time to help her prepare.

We were so pleased for Carrie. She was called to go to Salvador, in Brazil. *How significant*, I thought to myself, *that*

Mehr

she will teach the Gospel of Jesus Christ in Salvador, the Spanish word for Savior. She's happy to be going and she's happy with her life. When she returns, she'll have one more year of college and will know what she wants to do with her life.

As if Carrie's mission weren't enough of a reason to decline, I had just been asked to be the Relief Society President of our Ward. I had lived thirty years as an adult trying to be a good "disciple." I want to please the Lord and obey his commandments, although I've had ample experience with repentance. I've taught Primary children and tried to help others. I have seven children, for crying out loud!

Some people think that I'm just plain stupid because I never wanted a career outside my home. I'm not a sprinter. It was all I could do when my children were younger to cope with what was required of me as a mother. I didn't do many extras: I'm not a craft queen like some of my neighbors; the house is never spotless; I never went back to school for an advanced degree. I did make time for myself when necessary, taking community education classes in orchestra, continuing my lifelong love of the cello, upholstery, computer and communication. I taught classes in literature, self-esteem, French. I have managed to keep busy.

So, the thought of a big birthday party did not throw me into paroxysm of joy. But, I got on board. Aunt Glad and I reserved a park "gazebo" near her home in Salt Lake, to accommodate my Uncle Hugh who had become increasingly disabled from heart failure. We sent out notices even though Mom kept trying to cancel the party, protesting that it was too much bother. Finally, I told her that we were having it whether she was coming or not. She came.

I made tons of "sloppy Joe," in honor of my Grandma Reid, who always brought her own special recipe to picnics. Judy cut up fresh vegetables, Marilyn bought stuff for decorations, and Den had a mid-life crisis and couldn't make it. I love my brother dearly, but he can never find his way to Utah. In all, nearly thirty-five people showed up and Mom was very pleased. Gracie came all the way from New York, Dad's nephew Erwin arrived early and regaled us with stories of the "old days," Nate and Buffy brought my fifth grandchild. Gracie and I had bought t-shirts for Mom and her cousin Hazel who had also just turned 80, saying "Hot Mama." They loved them!

Mehr

Was all this a sacrifice? Hell, no, a privilege! It was an honor for me to honor my mother. She, who had given over half a century to me, trying to guarantee my own chances for happiness. And, I am happy. Sure, I've known great pain, but also great joy. Who am I? I'm the product of example. My ancestors made enormous sacrifices for their faith. They, too, had joy, perhaps in more limited ways than I have. My Dad taught me one thing very well: be who you are and do not worry about the disapproval of fools. Dad refused to be a victim, always preferring to find some solution to any problem, if he could. He realized early that he couldn't tolerate authority, so he started his own business. I hope I've taught my own children to cope as well. I've tried to teach them how to be happy, unselfish and kind. (Some day, they'll see I was pretty darned smart.)

Once again, Gracie read poetry. Our 4'10" sister from Buenos Aires stood on a chair under the shadow of the Wasatch Mountains and read her own tribute to Mother in Spanish. The sight of this small woman perched on a picnic bench under the shadow of the Wasatch speaking in a language at once soft and beautiful, but totally incomprehensible to her, touched Mother and brought tears. Finally, she could weep.

****

Judy:

I didn't particularly want to travel from Texas for this party, either. My trips to Utah always seemed loaded with cluster bombs of guilt and anger. My Aunt Gladys wanted to know why I hadn't visited her, my sister Nance was angry that I wasn't helping prepare the food for the picnic and my cousin Ron was just waiting to provoke me with some put-down. Why do I fall for it, every time? He is almost the same age as I am, a middle child himself, insecure about his ability and his accomplishments, and he dishes me about the way my kids speak Spanish. Of course, I defend them, get into a row, but why bother?

It's all too much, the heavy sentiment, the overwhelming heat, the contentious cousin, so I just retreated, fanned myself with a paper plate and stared at those incredible mountains. *How did they get those wagons through the canyonss?* I

Mehr

wondered, as I always did when I saw the great crevasses between the mountains.

So, what now, in the saga of this dysfunctional family, and what family is not? I don't think that our family was particularly dysfunctional. Sure, our polygamous great-grandparents died early, making my grandmother an orphan. Yes, I think Grandpa Reid had secrets, some early sexual liaison, or so the rumor goes. And our Swiss immigrant grandparents? I don't imagine there was love in that match. Grandma Mehr shaved Grandpa Mehr every morning, like a servant. But, I'd be naive not to think there were many loveless marriages on the frontier, as well as rough times.

As for our parents, Mom and Dad, I really do think that they loved each other at times, but neither of them brought out the best in the other. The last ten years of Dad's life amounted to a tortuous ordeal for both of them and maybe by the time he died, all the love had been spent. *How is that different from other families?*

What I want to feel, what I must feel, is a sense of forgiveness. I need to forgive Dad for wrongs, real or imagined, so I can dump the baggage and fly again. He was generous in wanting all the treasures of heaven and earth to be heaped upon his children, and he heaped all he could himself. He wanted us to share his religious beliefs, even though his own were often peppered with hypocrisy. He wanted us to laugh heartily and enjoy life with all its inequities. He had a strong testimony of the living Christ who lives in us as we do His work. He was at times a very good, compassionate, loving and gentle father and at others, a very cruel man.

I want to believe that he is redeemed, that his faults and weaknesses have been stripped away and he is now the gentle father in heaven that he had always hoped to be. That image is the one I would now like to preserve while I let the rest go. I love you, Daddy and I forgive you, Judy

****

Dennis:

No, I didn't go to the reunion, but I thought about all of them, my sisters and my relatives. Mostly, I thought about Dad. He was never a happy man and he probably wouldn't be happy that I closed the shop, but times change and so does the economy. After twenty-five years of working behind that counter, I am free and I love every minute of it. At last I can feel something called joy. These aren't the best of times in my life, financially, but they are the best of times I've ever had. I can enjoy life and I'm not restricted by work. Dad wouldn't have understood what I'm doing because his work was his life. He grew up in the Depression, started a family in the middle of World War II—a guy, with four kids, he couldn't have even thought about not working.

There should be a trigger in life, a time when you trip over the wire and your realize it's time to quit. There wasn't for me, so I made my own. When the business went downhill after he died, I struggled, but finally, let it go. For the first time in my adult life I have time to sit under a tree in my backyard, read a book and feel the sunshine on my face. I feel that at last I've found myself.

****

Marilyn:

There we all were in the blazing sun of an August afternoon in Utah, at least those of us who were still left, those of us still able to remember the ghosts of uncles who were fighter pilots in World War II, of grandmothers who were daughters of polygamous parents, of aunts who blemished the family name with too many boyfriends and fatherless children. We, the sons and daughters of George Henry Shaffer of the Augustus Wagon Train, departing Council Bluffs on June 14, 1862 in the company of Captain Henry Miller, who met and married my great, great grandmother, Esther Ann Jessup at the foot of Emigration Canyon, were gathered beneath the trellises of Kimball Park overlooking the I-15, to celebrate Mother's 80th Birthday.

As the oldest child of my parents, Al and Vivian, the oldest grandchild of my grandparents, Roy and Marcia Reid and Edward and Lena Mehr, I joined them in this dry, parched desert. We gathered, the progeny of those hardy souls who swam the Platte River lashed to wagon trains, pushed their loaded handcarts 1800 miles over the plains of Iowa and Kansas and through the mountains of Wyoming and Idaho until they reached the spare, dry valley of the Great Salt Lake. They who watched their mothers and fathers and loved ones die of tuberculosis and influenza just kept on marching. In the evening, on the open plains under the stars, they danced to the

Mehr

strums of guitar strings, then shivered in their woolen blankets, resisting the dense cold, fearing the approach of Indians who always watched from the nearby hills. In the morning, they packed their belongings onto wagons and handcarts and continued their march to the Great Salt Lake Valley.

Who were we, those of us sitting on picnic benches under these vine-covered trellises? We were the progeny of Henry's granddaughter, Marcia Porter, who had been orphaned at 13. We were Marcia's children, grandchildren, great grandchildren, well-accustomed to all the luxuries of the late twentieth century. We were also the progeny of her husband, Royal Reid, the son of itinerant Irish preachers. We drank soda from plastic cups, ate chicken grilled over charcoal briquettes purchased at Wal Mart's, spread our paper tablecloths over the park tables now neatly etched with logos from Salt Lake's graffiti artists. Here we gathered to honor Marcia and Roy Reid's oldest daughter, Vivian, "Querida Vivian," as Gracie called her.

Once again, Gracie read poetry in her native Argentinian tongue, dynamic and impassioned, a musical tribute. Our 4'10" sister from Buenos Aires stood on a chair under the shadow of

BROKEN CIRCUITS
A Memoir of Alzheimer's Disease in Four Voices

the Wasatch Mountains and offered a tango to her adopted mother, "Vivian Querida."

Querida Vivian, dressed in a turquoise jogging suit, tried to enjoy the attentions bestowed upon her with embarrassed winks at her audience and smiles through moments of foggy synapses as she struggled to recall the names of a new generation of children. She did her best to enjoy the love that they and her "adopted" Argentinian daughter held for her in their hearts.

Under these trellises we have gathered, cousins well-fed in our middle-age, surrounded by blonde children eager for slices of chocolate cake. Our "adopted" father, Uncle Hugh arrived late, tethered to his oxygen tank and gasping as he spoke. He looked drawn and weak, reminding us all of our own maturing and warning us of the imminent loss of this mammoth old tree-trunk that now rooted us to the earth. Dad was there, too, in the shadows under the trellises, watching and taking silent note. His nephew, Erwin, recalled the old days, how as young men, he and Dad had sold knit dresses to prostitutes in San Bernardino, still blushing at the memory. Dad was there still, lingering, filtering into conversation,

Mehr

touching memories, calling us back to other times, connecting the broken circuits. He was there. Every minute.

***

POSTSCRIPT

East Hampton, New York

June 2003

In the past eight years since our father died, we four children, Nancy Snell, Judy Olson, Dennis Mehr, and myself, Marilyn Mehr, have continued to grow closer and become a loving family. Writing this book challenged us in ways we could not have imagined. We argued, cried, withdrew and then revised and wrote some more.

The other large challenge we faced was caring for our mother, Vivian. We expected her to "bounce back," after Dad's death, reconnect with friends, her music and former interests. Little did we know that she, too, would slowly, but inevitably, succumb from the ravages of Alzheimer's disease. We transferred the lessons we had learned in caring for our father to providing better care for her. When Mother was unable to live alone, she moved to Texas to live with Judy's daughter, Karin, for a year and a half. Then, she spent the next two years in an Alzheimer facility in Salt Lake City, near Nancy and her family, as well as her sister, Gladys Snyder. She died there on August 24, 2002.

As for her children, we have connected many of the "broken circuits" of our childhood and tried to live whole lives as adults. My sister Nancy still resides in Utah, but travels frequently with her husband Lee, visiting children and exploring new areas of the world. Judy has been promoted to a full-time faculty position at Sam Houston State University, has lost weight, and enjoys spending time with her husband and grandchildren. Dennis, still lives with his wife Linda in Fullerton, California. He has closed the auto parts shop in Bell Gardens, learned to play golf and attends AA weekly. I've made a few changes, as well. After three years at the University of Kentucky, Betty and I moved to East Hampton, New York, where we are active in political and cultural organizations, teach part-time and and write. We are all leading full and satisfying lives.

ABOUT THE AUTHORS

MARILYN MEHR, Ph.D., is presently a part-time professor at Baruch College of the City University of New York, a psychologist and writer. Formerly, she was a Professor of Family Medicine, at the University of Kentucky Medical School as well as Chair of the Department of Health Psychology, at the California School of Professional Psychology, in Los Angeles.

For several years, Dr. Mehr maintained a large clinical practice devoted primarily to family counseling. Many of her clients have been older adults, some of them afflicted with Alzheimer's and dementias. She has presented widely in the medical and psychological community on issues of family dynamics, women's health, as well as gay and lesbian medical care.

In 1993, she co-authored *The Courage to Achieve,* with her partner of thirty-three years, Dr. Betty Walker. She has also completed a novel, WHITEROCKS, based upon the experience of Mormon immigrants in Utah in the early 1900's. She is Co-President of the Universalist Unitarian Congregation of the South Fork, in Long Island, New York, where she also sings in the choir.

NANCY ANN MEHR SNELL is the mother of seven children and lives in Highland, Utah, with her husband, Lee. She is also the grandmother of fifteen—ten boys and five girls. She works part-time as a secretary for the Alpine/Highland Police Department in Alpine, Utah. She has taught high school French and English and is a graduate of Brigham Young University. Additionally, she has been the editor of *The Highland Piper,* a community newspaper, for five years. As a member of the Church of Jesus Christ of Latter-Day Saints (Mormon), she was Relief Society President for three-and-a half years, but is happy at this time to be a teacher in the Primary Organization for ten-year old boys.

JUDITH E. MEHR OLSON, Ph.D., currently teaches in the Department of Language, Literaracy and Special Populations, at Sam Houston State University, in Huntsville, Texas, where she has lived with her husband and four children for over thirty years. For ten years, she was the founding Director of the Learning Assistance Center, where she developed and implemented programs for immigrant English language students. With her husband, James, she has authored a book about Cuban-Americans. She has served two terms as Relief Society President of her local Latter-Day Saint congregation. Her adult children and twelve grandchildren continue in the footsteps of their parents and grandparents to learn, to achieve and to serve.

DENNIS REID MEHR is the son of Alma and Vivian Reid Mehr and has served proudly and honorably in the United States Air Force during the Vietnam War. Upon his return, he successfully managed Mehr Distributing Company with his father. While he has traveled widely, he has always called California his home, where he remained near his parents during their later years. His education in the school of life has been broad and varied. He both admired and worked beside people who took little for granted and made their own opportunities. He and his wife, Linda Brunelle, are the parents of two children and two grandchildren, who delight and enchant them. He is currently in the enviable position of playing golf whenever he wishes.

Printed in the United States
139715LV00001B/211/A